My Crown
of
Beauty for Ashes

Thitu Kariba

Nsemia

First Edition: 2014
Second Edition: 2017

Published by Nsemia Inc. Publishers (www.nsemia.com)
Oakville, Ontario, Canada
Printed and Distributed in Kenya by Nsemia (K) Limited.

Edited by: Wanjiru Marima
Cover Concept & Illustration: Adrian Yongo
Cover Design: Danielle Pitt
Layout Design: Bethsheba Nyabuto
Law consultant: Macharia King'ori
Cover photography by: Emmanuel Jumbo
Hair and make-up by: Mark Allan Karanja
Dress by: Achieng Melisa

Note for Librarians:
A cataloguing record for this book is available from Library and Archives Canada and Kenya National Library.

ISBN: 978-1-926906-39-3

"When I look at myself in the mirror today, I don't recognize myself anymore. Instead of something ugly and loathsome, I see something beautiful and worthy. I am not defined by what others say, or even what the media says. When I look in the mirror today, I see the image and likeness of God. I see the great I AM. I see a child of God. When I look in the mirror and ask who is the fairest of them all, I see you and I. I guarantee that if you stand in front of your mirror and ask the same thing you will see yourself, too."

Thitu Kariba
Nairobi, June 2014

Table of Contents

Introduction

When I think about my life's journey, the things I have come across and the experiences I have had, I am blown away. I know that there are over seven billion people on this planet. But do we really appreciate that out of the seven billion; no two of them are the same? Do we realize that although there is nothing new under the sun, none of the seven billion people can experience, feel, express and learn the same way? Do we realize that although there are over seven billion people on this planet, we are all originals?

Most of us go through life not taking note of and not appreciating our uniqueness. However, it is not entirely our fault. We are born into systems that try to make societies homogenous. Such groups are generally easier to manage and control.

Which brings me to this point; I never wanted to write this book. I got a call from a lady in the United States who suggested I do it. I demurred. I have a social media page that this lady happened to come across. Being Kenyan and with a passion for helping young Kenyan girls, she felt the need to reach out and urge me to tell my story. That is how I took interest in turning my story into a book. We had one long telephone conversation and a few e-mail exchanges and that was it. We have never met nor do I know her beyond that. She was simply the seed planter.

After the seed was planted, my hesitation persisted. It was not until I tried to help a teenager who had been pregnant several times under the influence of drugs, that I knew I had to speak up. The young lady was expectant again. This may have been the fifth time. She wanted to keep the child, but she was also a child and she came from a family where reputation mattered most.

After the holidays the following year, I tried to reach out to her to help, but I was informed that she had died. I was distressed and I wanted to know the circumstances surrounding her death. I learnt that she committed suicide, but the family had covered this fact up. They did not want suicide linked to their family. I also learnt that her siblings had been badly impacted as a result of her death. I feared it would be a vicious cycle.

Silence is powerful. It has the power to kill by allowing bad things that happen to continue happening.

Although it was too late for this particular lady, it was not too late for others in similar circumstances. I resolved to break the taboo associated with mental health and suicide. I knew I was treading on delicate grounds. However, I was determined to put my ego aside, lay my own life bare and even risk putting my reputation on the line if it would mean another suicide would be avoided.

I hereby present my life as an open book. This is my real life testimony and it is my prayer that He will give you, too, a crown of beauty for ashes.

Accolades

"If openness and eagerness to learn from other people's lives and experiences is what you yearn for, this is the book you need. Thitu Kariba is the first person we have met who is willing to bring out her inner convictions, emotional fights and abuse in order to fulfill her life's purpose. This purpose is to heal those around her and the world as a whole. God bless you in your search for healing."

Mike Mutenyo, Gospel Musician

VKP Music Group

Break the Silence:
The Healing Path of Sexual and Other Abuse

Research by counselling psychologists and communication specialists shows that sexual abuse occurs in one in every four families all over the world. Girls often bear the brunt of this abuse. Many children do not know how to deal with the shocking, unbelievable and traumatic events. When adults receive the unbearable news of their children's sexual molestation, more often than not, they either deny it or warn their children against talking about it. It becomes a family secret. Indeed, many African traditions have sayings and proverbs implying that domestic issues are not for public consumption. Unfortunately, the more issues are bottled up, the more they cause psychological, physical and even spiritual damage.

Without intervention, survivors of sexual abuse may carry a deep sense of shame and unnecessary self-blame, guilt and hatred. They also tend to feel helpless and powerless. In the end, it becomes a vicious cycle that eats them from inside. Pause for a minute and think of the story of Tamar in 2 Samuel 13. Tamar was raped by her step-brother Amnon. What did her real brother, Absalom, tell her after the incident? He urged her to keep it to herself. So Tamar remained silent and desolate in her brother's house. Tamar withdrew to a life of obscurity and isolation.

In my view, sexual abuse is like having a deep cut on one's wrist. Imagine putting a covering over the wound without attending to it; it becomes infectious! Like other traumatic experiences, sexual abuse leaves a big emotional and psychological scar in the victim's life. For healing to occur, the wound must be opened, cleaned gently and the cut sown up, one stitch at a time. Although with time the wound would heal, the scar will remain.

"A heart at peace gives life to the body," says Solomon in the book of Proverbs. When peace is robbed through sexual abuse, the whole person is affected. I urge our society to take the bold step to not only condemn the culprits but to also offer support to the victims. One way to support is through counselling or offering a safe and conducive environment where they can openly be listened to as they share their experiences and accorded the necessary support. In Psalm 32:3, King David said, "When I kept it all inside, my bones turned to powder, my words became day long groans." It is time to gather courage, break the silence and speak it out! Congratulations Thitu.

Julia Kagunda
June 2014

Chapter 1
My Garden Flower

I love flowers. It is amazing how effortlessly glorious they are. Every shade, petal, design and shape; every intricate detail of any flower seems to have been so masterfully calculated and put together. Sometimes I wonder how God does it. How did He know that the brown colour of the soil would blend with the green colour of the leaves, or that that particular shade of purple was just right? This makes me wonder at times if He took as much care in putting me together as He did with His other creations. If He, indeed, did take as much care in creating me, why would He let anything mess up that which He created: did He not have much use for me? Was I of less value than others or was it that He was too busy with more important creatures?

It may be difficult for you to understand why I ask such a thing and, more so, at such a young age. I was only a child, no more than ten years, when these thoughts would tread in the pool of my mind.

As a little girl, it was usual to find me outside sitting amongst the blossoms of flowers that sprang from the fruitful African soil. In all my collection of colour pencils, I had never seen such variety of colours as I did in the flower garden. It is no wonder that I loved spending so much time there. I recall plucking some petals and sticking them on a picture I had drawn just to have that exact shade of pink. I even recall how I would lick and stick the bright coloured red petals on my fingernails and pretend I was some elegant movie star with dashing long nails.

I recall the sweet nectar I would suck from some of the flowers that draped the hedges around our home. Not only were they beautiful, but they were also sweet. Yet all they did was to just be the flowers they were! I wonder how they do it: how they are just beautiful without make up; how they smell so sweet without wearing expensive fragrances; and how they taste so sweet with no sugar added. Being outside, playing in the garden of flowers, I felt I had found my place, because for the first time I too felt like a garden flower.

Each day the gardener would allow me to water the flowers. He would let me touch them, pick them and even eat them when curiosity got the better of me. He loved the flowers; he cared for them and he treated me just like he did each one those flowers.

We loved to play doctor when we were done tending the garden. He would play the doctor and I, the patient. He would attend to me with a flower in his hand to make me feel better and I always did.

Some days, I would pretend I had a cold, other days that I had fallen while playing on the swings. Whatever the case was, he was always ready to 'treat' me and 'prescribe' the perfect flower to go with it.

One day, I noticed something was different in his conduct. His touch was different. His voice was different and he did not have a flower. He told me that I was his flower and he wanted to care for me even more than he cared for any flower.

He leaned over and took in the scent of me as I had seen him do with the flowers in the garden. He placed his lips on my skin as he made his way down my juvenile frame. Thinking about it, I wonder how he could not see that I was not a woman. I was only a small girl.

"You smell just like a flower, your skin is so soft like the rose petals. It is sweet like honey," he said.

I have tried many times to understand what it was that he may have seen in me that gave him the impression that

I was anything other than a child. We just did not fit. His body weighed down so heavily on top of mine that I could hardly breathe. Could he not see this? I wondered!

The gardener put his hands on me, and in me. I never knew there were places in me to go into until he went there with his hands. I burned with a pain that felt like a fire in my soul. It went beyond the physical, extending to an innermost part of my being that I never knew existed.

Ignorance would have been my bliss at this point. There are things a child should never know, yet I was made familiar with. There are things in a man that a child, a little girl should never see, but not only was I forced to see, I was also forced to experience them. Yet even then, he gave me something I did not have much of – time and attention. In my childish mind it seemed like love and affection.

My father often travelled; when he did, I missed him terribly. As time passed, whenever he would travel I would fall ill. It goes without question that when the cat is away the mice would play, and play they did. As I recall it now, the gardener would have his friend come over to play with us too. It was not long before I had to see a real doctor because I would burn every time I went for a short call.

There are things a child should be ignorant of in order to have a blissful childhood. I did not have the privilege of ignorance or the bliss that came with it. Although I was just a child, a part of me fed off all the attention. The gardener and his friend told me I was beautiful. They said I was special, even though I did not like what they did. It hurt. But someone was around with me and for me and at the time, that is what counted. Not every adult was too busy and absent.

It was not long before things began to change. I began to spend more time with him and less time with the flowers. I began to fall ill more often. I began to burn more too. I already detested the thought that other men might notice me. I began to wish I were a boy. I started dressing like one hoping that they would see me as one of them, and that way, they would not touch me.

I wonder if Mum and Dad saw it. Did they notice the change? The sickness? Maybe they were too busy. I know Dad was hardly there, but without saying a word, I know that I was silently screaming and shouting out to anyone who would take the time to see. No one ever did.

As an adult, I don't think there is a good reason one can give as to why I did not come out and say something. No one ever told me what to do if a grown man ever did what the gardener did. I'll tell you this, if someone had told me, I would have done as I would have been told.

This world is full of people who do unfathomable things. I am sure no parent would ever think it could happen to their child even though we know for sure it happens. My ignorance, and that of my parents, was the gardener's bliss. I know for sure that, though we may not want our children to know that such things happen, keeping them ignorant is just what abusers hope for and prey on.

It is not a comfortable subject to discuss with a child, but I assure you allowing your children to know that grownups should not touch them in certain areas in certain ways can be a protective measure. It is important for children to be able to tell you if anyone ever does. That would allow us all to sleep comfortably.

Comfort comes at the price of discomfort. We have to be willing to be uncomfortable and talk about these things even with little children if we want to have peace of mind.

We have to keep our eyes open and our ears free of noise to hear and see our children change or fall sick in unusual ways and times. We have to be able to hear them even when they are screaming out in silence.

What happened to me as a child left me with many fears as I discovered later in life. I feared being a girl. I feared being beautiful and attractive. I feared the male reproductive organ.

As I grew older, I was not aware of what had happened to me. I was never completely aware of the full effects of their actions and my mind seemed to have blocked out much of it for many years. It was only when I was older when certain things were said, and certain smells encountered that feelings were triggered. I cannot say for sure what triggered a memory, but I would realize something was not right. For a while, I thought many of the flashes I got were dreams only to realize they were not. There are things I know are lost in my mind forever. But there are also new things that I discover even now.

As these memories come, I don't suppress them. I allow them to come and I allow the feelings to flow. What I do not allow is a reaction. I take time to understand that none of it was my fault. I take time to understand that the person who did it was also not an everyday person. Doing this allows me to forgive any part of me that still feels that I am partly to blame. It allows me to still have trust in people knowing that not all are that way.

There is the one who breaks and the one who puts back together. The one who stays broken and the one who chooses to heal. I may not have had a choice then, but I have a choice now. That is how my past will affect my present. It took me a while to know that and even choose but it's not too late for you, too, to choose.

People will continue to do the things they do to us only if we allow them. The past can be a very present thing if you choose to carry it with you. I had carried my childhood, or lack of it, for too long. I had to set it down, but not before it broke me down.

The choice to forgive and forget is one we need to learn to make out of necessity and not out of privilege. One we need to make because we want to live and not because we are afraid to die.

Do parents realize they cannot be there all the time for their children? A parent is not God and that's alright. Children go through various stages of development. At around the age of six, girls tend to talk and keep company more with men or with their dads while boys tend to talk more and keep company with women or their mums. This is very normal and you should not stop it for fear of abuse. Instead, supervise it. Even better, be the one available for your child. If you cannot be there all the time, ensure you make the time. Remember time is not found, it is made. If you don't make time to love and play with your child, others will.

I have heard of several cases of house helps and aunts abusing little boys. It is not just the girl-child who is in danger of abuse. In such cases, it is about informing your child. Let them know their bodies and what is acceptable and what is not acceptable to do with others. Parents need to take time to bathe their children themselves, which is when you can notice changes, bruises and other things hidden under clothes.

Schools as well have a responsibility to teach child safety. We have heard of teachers, religious leaders and other care givers abusing students. This shows that abusers can be anywhere. An abuser could be anyone.

In the event that your child confides in you, anger and violence is not the response. Calling the child a liar or punishing them is just wrong. They need to trust you and you need to trust them. Ask yourself, "Why would my child make up such a story?" Believe your child first, even if it pits you against your spouse or other family members.

Children who are sexually abused tend to act more grown up in the way they talk, dress and behave. They will tend to hang out with their abusers and yet be fearful of them. They will tend to withdraw from playing with other children, dress differently either to enhance their looks or hide their bodies. They may even disallow you to bathe them for fear of something being seen. Understand that a child abuser has mind control over the child. The abuser usually tells the child 'nice' things and gives gifts that make the child feel special. An abuser may issue a threat to the child. It is therefore up to us as parents and guardians to look beyond the surface. Support the child regardless of how outrageous their claim may sound. Understand that child abuse, sexual or otherwise is a crime and it is your duty, as a parent or guardian, to report it to law enforcement officers.

Chapter 2
My First Kiss

Many are the great stories told about firsts. I have heard fascinating stories about that special first kiss. Although that has not been the case for me, I do enjoy hearing about how green the grass is on the other side of the fence. Some may think, when you are around people who have gone through hard times, talking about your good times in their presence is selfish. However, whenever you are in a storm, it is always nice to hear about sunny skies. It gets you out of your funk and allows you to see where you can and could be. That way, when you are down, you don't need more bad news or stories.

I recall sitting with girls in school, and even at home, and we would all share our boy-stories. It was always fun. I felt like I was at the right age at the right time for the subject. Girls talked about their first kiss and when it happened. I would tell them about my first kiss – a version that would be similar and acceptable to them, but never the whole truth.

After my experience with the gardener, I learnt that with each person, each painful encounter, a part of me died. With the gardener I always felt like he exposed me to other men like him, so that wherever I went, men would see me the same way he saw me – as though I had been tagged or marked for abuse.

Because my father was a frequent traveller, the rest of us would go to my auntie's house often. I enjoyed the company of my cousins, though they were older than my brother and I. They were very cool. My aunt was a blast too and a part of me always wanted to be like her. The thing I loved most about her, even from such a young age, was that she was doing it all by herself. She was divorced. She was living a good life as a single parent. From my point of view, which was a few feet off the ground, her life was everything I wanted.

My cousin, Tom, always had his friends over, and I really never paid much attention to them. After all, they were older and I preferred to steer clear of that type. I was also just a kid and so they had all these rules like how I was not allowed in their room, how I could not watch what they did and so on. It was great and annoying at the same time being a kid. You got treated like one when you wanted to be treated like a grownup. On the other hand, you got treated like a grownup when you wanted to be treated like a kid.

Whenever my cousin's friends came around and they allowed us to hang out together, I got to learn all the new cool dances and got exposed to great music. I recall singing along to Tracy Chapman, Bob Marley, UB40, George Michael, Michael Jackson, and many more.

From a young age, I loved music. Whenever my father was around, we would put on one of his Ray Charles records, listen to some Jackson Five, sing along and dance and be in pure bliss. It is amazing the joy that one can experience in those four minutes of a great song especially while dancing with your dad.

Admiration for my aunt and the blissful company of my cousins made my aunty's house a place where I wanted to be. We went over almost every weekend, and I got all the attention in the world from my loving aunt, which was what I craved. Nothing would pass her. Not a scratch on my body or a sneeze. I never went to bed without a mug of hot sweetened milk. Something about milk just makes life that much better. To this day, I cannot go through a day without milk, although now I prefer it with coffee or tea as opposed to just warm and sweet.

I remember how on some days I would sit on the couch and watch cartoons as I waited for my aunt to make me something to eat or as I waited for her to get the bath water ready for me. My cousin and his friends would sometimes come and sit with me for a few minutes as they made their way from the kitchen, if not the toilet and back to the room where they used to hang out.

This was a kind gesture on their part that although I could not go into the room as I was just a kid, they had not forgotten I was around.

"I got you all your favourite movies to watch so you will not get bored. If you need anything just knock on the door," my cousin's friend would tell me.

This particular day, my cousin's friend came and sat with me. His name was Flavian but we all called him Flavour. He asked me the usual questions such as what I had been watching, how I had been, and if I needed anything from the kitchen. After I assured him that I was fine, he got up to leave. However, when he got to the door, he turned around and walked back to me. He asked me to stick out my tongue. I resisted for a while. I thought he was playing a silly game that I was not interested in. I just wanted to watch TV.

After pleading with me for a while, I resolved that doing what he asked would be the fastest way to get rid of him. That way, I could go back to my cartoons. He leaned over and took my tongue in his mouth. It felt slow and torturous, though I am sure, it did not happen as slowly as it seemed. Each second seemed like an eon. His tongue tasted of cigarettes and alcohol. I know this because at the time my father used to smoke and drink and, when he was not in, I would taste his drink and play with his cigarettes.

It was the foulest taste in the world, and my tongue in his mouth was the weirdest and most disgusting feeling I had felt to date.

"That is a French kiss. It is special and for sophisticated ladies like you. I do not kiss everyone like that," he said. He smiled and winked at me playfully.

From that very moment on, all I could think of was how much I suddenly hated him. I detested him, not only for what he had just done to me, but also for what he would likely do in future.

Sadly, it happened to me in what was supposed to be my safe haven; the one place I was happy to be a child.

He got up and told me how much he had enjoyed the act and how sweet I tasted, all the while smiling from ear to ear.

I wanted to cry but I could not. I shuddered when I imagined the plans he had for me! I could see how his mind worked, and that made me afraid and tired. I was afraid because, unlike the gardener, this guy was allowed into the house. He was younger and wild. I was tired because I was not an adult and I was tired of being treated like one. I just wanted to relax in front of the TV, and watch cartoons like other kids.

"I'll come by tomorrow and we can watch something together," he said. "Is there any particular movie I can bring for us to watch?"

"Auntie has already got me all the ones I wanted. She promised she would watch with me tomorrow. I'll tell her you are coming so we can wait for you and watch together," I said hoping he would not come. Surely, he could not do what he wanted with me while my aunt was around.

Although I loved my aunt, I did not want to tell her what had happened to me. I blamed myself. I felt that I was somehow responsible. Indeed, it was not the first time it had happened. I thought that I must have done something to make him see me as he did, leading him to kiss me.

I had another reason to be apprehensive. I knew that there would be trouble between my aunt and cousins should they become aware, consequences of which I was not prepared for. I could not imagine not being able to visit my aunt's house anymore. I resolved to pay the price. In any case, I was convinced I was at fault.

This was a time in my life when I felt that, although I had choices, it was always between bad and worse. I did not feel that I had a choice for better. It may have all been due to my age as well. I was a child who should never have had to make such choices. The choices I made allowed him to keep doing to me things that I did not like.

In the fullness of time, I have come to realize that every decision we make carries with it both short and long term effects. For instance, the decision to terminate a pregnancy, in the short term means one is no longer pregnant. In the long run though, it could mean that you could never get pregnant again.

My choice to remain quiet was made easier by the fact that, at the time, I felt I had nothing to lose or gain. The things the perpetrator did to me had already been done. Indeed, whether he did them or not, I would still be a rose with thorns.

I was already touched, defiled and ruined. There was nothing anyone could do to change that.

I was a child. Speaking up meant I would have everyone know what had happened to me. It would mean that the little that was left of my childhood, and the bit of normalcy I still had, would be no more.

*****

On most days, my cousin and his friends were out and about and so was I. I liked going out to sit at my grandparents' grave site. No one ever came there. I would go into the forest and to the stream to just be. I was attracted by the quiet, tranquil atmosphere of these places.

I often got into trouble for this. However, whether I got into trouble when I got back did not concern me. No spanking could outdo the other thing that may have been waiting for me when I got back.

Initially, Flavour would come, sit and talk with me. He would then proceed to kiss me and leave. As time went by, he realized that I was not reporting the matter. He took it further.

He would sit with me and proceed to touch me over my clothes as he simultaneously touched himself. I was thankful that it was over my clothes and not on my skin. This happened when my aunt would be out of the house. But it did not happen in a closed room, but right there in the living room, in front of the TV.

I recall how Flavour would jump whenever my cousin called his name or the kitchen door opened. I would laugh at him inwardly thinking what a fool he was and how he was going to get caught, eventually.

I think some of what scared him about me was that I was not afraid of him or of what he was doing. I knew the drill and went along with it. I even guided him along the way at times. There was a part of me that would inwardly say, "No dummy, do it like this."

I recall the first time I saw a man making love. I was only a child and it was so confusing. It seemed painful and I thought that they were sick. I likened it to the case of an epileptic girl I had seen in our school.

I wondered why it caused them to be sick. As time passed, I realised it wasn't sickness but pleasure. Something about me made them feel good and have this weird reaction. In some way, I felt powerful and in other ways I felt like I was possessed by a man-controlling demon. Whatever I had, men seemed to want. And they seemed willing and able to give me anything I wanted for it: trips into the city, all the ice cream I could eat and more.

As time progressed my cousin's friend got bolder and eventually made it to under my clothes. He also got smarter. He would come watch TV with me, hold me on his lap and cover me with a blanket. This was not unusual because it was sometimes cold. We would watch TV for a while before he did anything. It was as though he was allowing me to at least feel like a child and get my time to enjoy the TV show before he got started. He would then slip his hand under the blanket and touch my body.

As I sat on him I could feel how his body reacted to me. At first it scared me. With my childish imagination, I believed it was a snake. I stayed motionless because I thought if I reacted it would bite me.

This went on for a while. The worst or the craziest part is that he could do this in front of people and they would not suspect a thing.

Flavian was wild, and naughty. Although he was not one who could be trusted when it came to many other things, no one would suspect that he could do what he was doing to me. Perhaps he even shocked people by how sweet and caring he could be towards me. I am sure that is exactly what most child abusers appear to be: a guy who looks harmless and loves kids; one who reads to, plays with and is good with them.

I also comforted myself that my aunt's place was not where I would live forever. As such, I was not too bothered with the price I had to pay. It was also something I had learnt to numb myself from. I did not feel defiled anymore. I did not feel lost. I did not feel anything. I was dead inside.

The mind has its own way of protecting us because it was not until I was an adult that I began to remember these encounters. I would get visions that I thought were dreams. My therapist explained that they were repressed memories. They were memories of traumatic events that my mind had blocked out as a means of coping. I still do not have all my childhood memories.

One therapist offered to use hypnosis. This is an artificially induced state of relaxation and concentration in which deeper parts of the mind become more accessible. It is used clinically to reduce reaction to pain, to encourage free association on me and to bring them out. However, I was shaken by the idea that someone could have the power to put me in a state that was neither sleep nor consciousness but control my mind.

I felt controlled by something, demons or some evil for years and I did not need more of that. I felt that everyone everywhere wanted to control me in one way or the other: my body, my life, and now my mind.

There was something about hypnosis that seemed unnatural. I asked myself why, if my mind had blocked things out for my preservation, I would be forced to recall them. I had to trust that my mind had done what was best for me. I also felt at this point that after all the drugs and other forms of treatment I was undergoing, there had to be another way to find healing, peace and wholeness without taking such drastic and intrusive measures. I was not a Christian at the time. What many of the psychiatrists I saw offered felt more spiritual than mental.

I was not going to allow to be violated any further than I already had. I also did not have much trust in people. As such, I did not want to put my trust in the hands of anyone especially under the circumstances of hypnosis.

I would say that some things are best left in God's hands. He made me, my mind and I. He knows better than everyone how it works. I may not recall everything that has happened in the past, but that I can live with it.

Over the years, I have been able to recall one thing at a time and when I do, I take it to God in prayer. Forcing all the ghosts out at once could be too much. I trust that God is in control and He even gives us free will. I trust Him to take over my mind, my body and my soul, to heal me and to bring things to remembrance as He wishes.

Chapter 3
My Friend

The Bible says that there is a friend who sticks closer than a brother. True friendship is a rare and precious gem-should you ever find it. A friend is a term we often use casually. Now more than ever, in an ever changing world that has terminated the intimacy once shared by people in face-to-face encounters. Today all we have to do is get online, chat, text, no hand shake, no tone of voice and connection other than that to log into your internet to accept a friend request from a complete stranger.

People don't need to know each other anymore. One just needs to get on and look at your profile, find out where you come from, what school you went to, your favourite colour and a picture of what we can only hope is truly you if that is even your real name. This manifests just how far we have come technologically yet how far we have drifted from life, humanity, intimacy and living.

There was a time when I had a true friend. One I could see and touch. This friend wiped my tears and provided a shoulder to lean on. This is my account of such a time.

*****

Memories of my transitioning to secondary school are vivid. Yet it seemed just as I graduated from one level there was another to be started. My father would often say that school was important, that it would guarantee me a future and yet the future had seemed to have been robbed from me as a child in his very garden. Would school give back what I had lost?

School for me was not a place to be imparted with knowledge. It was a place to break free from the world I had come to know and be a child. I did not care for books. They made no sense to me. I did not care for numbers, they confused me.

I loved high school; the music room, the art room, the field and I especially loved the pool. I loved how you could hear nothing underwater and somehow the world and all the noise in it became a far off murmur. The water seemed to cool the burns not on my body, but my soul and floating was the closest I came to flying. I loved high school because I had found a place where I could get away from it all for hours a day and from days, a week. I could be a child and I could do childish things. I could get into trouble; I could get punished as a child. To me high school was like a part in a play that I enjoyed until the curtain came down and I had to go back to my reality.

I will never forget how a special new found friend touched me. It was unlike any other touch. I was wounded and hurt, and he touched me in a manner that did not break me more but lifted me up. Who knew there was such a thing within these beings called men? Or was it that he was not yet fully a man that he did not see and touch me as such? Could it be that what they saw, what I was to them remained hidden to him, at least for now?

He was tall, tall enough, it seemed, to touch the clouds upon which the heavens danced, and perhaps he was an angel. He was covered in sun-kissed skin, dipped in dark chocolate. His name was Atem. He had the most amazing voice, as sweet as the nightingale's song and soothing as a lullaby. He had a laugh that can only be called Isaac, for it was delight to listen to; it brought joy to me as Isaac did to Sarah. He had the smallest eyes yet they saw to the deepest part of me. One thing I could never forget was how his hand in mine was like a checkers board so different yet so perfectly suited. He was surely the finest of Jehovah's masterpieces. Oh, did I forget that he was an artist? He loved the art room and loved music and he had the most beautiful mind, filled with not just knowledge but wisdom and such creative and divine thoughts that sometimes I thought I was talking to God himself. If only I believed He existed at the time.

The idea that a merciful loving God existed was beyond what my heart could grasp for it had been torn apart by His beings. I recall being told that we had been made in His image and likeness but if this so-called God was anything like what I came to witness and know, I wanted nothing to do with Him. Many were the days I went to the church to hear of His goodness and mercies and never came to know what they were. For goodness' sake, had He no mercy on me? Was I not His child? I had also read in the good book that He had created some people for destruction and that was the only thing I came to understand. I finally knew my place in this creation and it lay in destructions, ruins and it seemed I was right on track.

My friend Atem was set apart. He was nothing like my abusers yet ordinary like us all. People fear what they do not understand and the other kids could not understand why Atem looked and talked the way he did. He was very tall, dark and energetic. He was awesome! I found myself right at home with him.

Having been touched by men in ways only reserved for a woman had run its course. I was not interested in the opposite sex. I did not fit in with the girls, who were all too excited 'uuh'-ing and 'aah'-ing about boys.

There was something about Atem that made it easy for me to get close to him. It was as though, in a way, I already knew him and instantly I loved him. It was a love that drew me to want the best for him. A love that drew me to want to protect him as he did me. A love that would have drawn me to pray for him and ask the angels to watch over him. It was a love that was pure, uncorrupted and young. It was a love that I was allowed to enjoy; a love befitting my age.

We spent so much time together. We talked all the time about everything. It was such an amazing friendship. I knew that I wanted it to be untouched by my darkness and so I never told him my secrets. It was the first time I was looked at with acceptance and adoration. He looked at me and treated me like a person who could do no wrong, who was flawless and perfect and it liberated me. Leaving home each day to spend the day in school with him was like living in wonderland. I could escape my hell and spend a few hours with one of heaven's angels and I just could not ruin that. He was my escape and secret hiding place.

I recall how he would wait for me in the mornings and we would ride in the bus to school together so we could sit and talk. I recall how I would get home and call him and keep talking till we had to get off the phone and get ready for another day in school. I recall how there were times I was so grateful that he did not like me the way other boys did. Though there were times I wished he would like me more than just a friend.

"Atem, you know we have been on the phone for over an hour again? We better get off before my mum realises, but I'll see you tomorrow morning," I said.

"Ok, I'll wait for you and save you a seat on the bus. Goodnight," he responded.

"Goodnight," I said.

It made me wonder now and then; we were so close and yet it seemed not close enough for him to like me that way. I wondered if anyone ever could. I was not like the other girls. Would I ever be treated or loved like one of them? I was smart enough to know not to dwell on such thoughts and moreover not to go on dreaming. I was not a dreamer, I dared not dream, but I was haunted by nightmares. Some people's dreams come true and my nightmares were my reality. I dared not to dream, there was nothing in it for me but time wasted and disappointment waiting.

I look back now and I am filled with a greater and deeper appreciation for my friend. I could write a library of books and all of them put together yet they could never truly say how grateful I am for him. I know that we were there for each other; I was to him what he was to me; a safe haven. I cannot begin to imagine what he was going through either – torn from his home, from his family, his father and never knowing about tomorrow, hoping and praying for peace in his home country and perhaps hoping that loss would not come knocking again. I do not know how he did it. How he could walk that path and still be who he was – gentle, kind and so loving.

I was silly around Atem. I do believe that with him, I truly become who I am. He freed me from the life I lived, the things I was forced to go through, and allowed me to just be who I truly was.

He made me laugh, I laughed with him and that was rare. It was never complicated. It was so natural, so easy as though it was just meant to be. I would get so mad when people gossiped trash about him.

*****

I was just a girl of 15 years. I had to make a choice to tell or not to tell my friend what I was going through. I had to count the cost. I knew that he, too, had a history. Atem still had so much to deal with. I chose not to add to that. He too was just a child. I know that many may feel all grown up while in high school but, at every stage in life there are things we get to experience that seem right for that time.

I was also glad that even though the stage was set for that high school sweetheart position, he never took it. The greatest gift Atem gave me was that of friendship at that time, because I never thought it possible for men or boys who got as close to me as he did to see me as just that. Perhaps he may have wanted more, but God knew I could not handle more and he too counted his costs and maybe having me as just his friend was far more valuable than a high school fling.

Chapter 4
My First

When we meet someone for the first time, or when we do, taste, hear something for the first time, it becomes engraved in your mind forever. I guess that's why they say that first impressions last forever. I recall sitting down with girls and trading stories of our firsts. Our first crush, our first time to be with a boy and so on. I would listen and wonder what it was like to experience things as they did. I would listen as theirs came to an end and my turn drew closer and eventually it came about the time to tell of my own. But how could I tell them of my first kiss? And how could I tell them of my first time when it was unlike any other? I couldn't and I wouldn't. Instead, I would borrow pieces of stories I had heard before the good, the bad and the ugly. With great craft of lying, I would add a little of my own creation and make up my own tales to tell.

"The other day, Peter walked me to my gate as usual, but this time, we took it further, to the door and when we realized there was no one home, he came in to keep me company. As we sat on the couch, he kissed me. It felt so magical. After that, we went to the room and before I knew it, we were all over each other. It was scary at first but, he knew just what to say to keep me calm. It was the best feeling in the world and all I can think about now is me and Peter in the room and when we will have that chance again," said Stacy.

I considered myself a virgin. Child abusers do not always have penetrative sex with a child, and because that was the case with me, I believed that I had not actually done anything and I was still considered a virgin. Maybe, it is something I just wanted to believe to make me feel less filthy, wasted and used. Maybe it was just the slight bit of hope that I held onto, something I knew I still had that had not been taken from me. It was something I cherished and something I wanted to give away to someone of my choosing. Some may disregard what I had endured as an abused child because there was no penetration, but it is very important to note that even without that, it is still sexual abuse and must be treated with the same level of condemnation.

High school was the time when we would go through many changes, and sex is one of the big things that is talked about. Some girls came close, others went all the way and then there was me who did not want to go anywhere near it. I wanted a long deserved break. I liked a few boys, and I knew what was on their mind which made me greatly disinterested in them instantly although, I still pretended to be. I was weird enough and I did not need more on my plate, so I played along when I had to. I did not really care for the friendship of the girls in school. All they ever did was talk about boys and I really needed a change of subject.

There was one boy who joined the school that I really liked. What I felt for him is not something I knew then how to put in words. It was not sexual or physical, or any other thing, but it was like a force that seemed to ignite and enlighten the whole of me. I never really thought or saw myself kissing him or anything of the sort, I was just drawn to him in some weird way. Regardless of what many may have thought, I left high school a virgin or at least just as I had entered it and I really did plan to stay that way.

When I told the story of my first, it was always different. He was Peter one time and John on the other. Every story I told about my first had something new and different, but how could I tell all these girls, that are sharing a milestone in their life with such celebration, about mine that I had not foreseen, planned or welcomed? One would think that telling the truth to girls like this would bring sympathy or empathy, but the truth in this case brings about rejection and isolation. You become that girl, the one people talk about, whisper about and the lies save us from the responses and reactions of people to your truth.

And then I turned 18. I had just gotten my driving licence and I was eager to learn and open my own restaurant and a chain of hotels. I did what I knew best which was getting a job and learn on the job. I had started working as early as at 17. I worked at a hotel in Nairobi. I would come in early, leave late and so on, as my shift demanded. I made friends quickly and easily. Whenever I needed to take a nap during the day or come in very early, I had a friend who could give me a luxurious room to do that. Because of my late working hours, my dad gave me a car to use. This particular night, I had made plans to do just that: come in from a night out, get some sleep, get up and get to work on time the next day. I worked hard and I made sure I was going to achieve my goals.

On this night, because I knew I had to go to work, I did not have anything to drink. I said bye to my friend and brother. As I made my way down Waiyaki Way, my car began to act up and stalled. It was in the wee hours of the night. I knew I could not stay in the car and especially on that road. It was dark and there was no one around I would go to for help. I managed to get the car off the road and made my way to the nearest bar. I then bumped into someone I had previously met in the clubs and told him my situation. He found me someone who could drop me off at the hotel, which was not far from where we were or his house.

His friend was not yet done with his drinks, and he invited me to sit and wait and ordered me a Coke. Halfway through my drink, I got up to go to the bathroom. Something we all do without giving it much thought. I got back, sat down and finished my drink. By the time I took my last sip, I was not myself. I do not even recall leaving the club or making it to the car, but I could hear them talking. They agreed that they could not drop me off at the hotel in my condition. I do not remember much about everything that happened.

"We can't drop this chick off like this. What are we supposed to say? No way I am getting in trouble for this. We better let her sleep it off and she can go in the morning," I heard one of them say.

It was a small dark clattered room. I think it was the servants' quarters. His friends were outside. He kept asking me if we could have sex and though I was not sober, I said no and pleaded with him not to do anything. This went on for a while and I began to lose consciousness as he was growing more and more frustrated. He decided he was tired of asking, but even in my state, I tried to put up a fight. I barely recall my hands being tied down. I do recall his voice, but the one thing I will never forget were his eyes. He was biracial and he had the most remarkable green eyes. On another day he would be that cute boy with the eyes, but here he was the green-eyed monster.

It is ironic that the thing I was avoiding when I chose not to wait in the car found me here in this little room with him forcing himself on me even when I said NO! He did not know or care that he was my first. I passed out and did not consciously experience all he did.

In the morning, I was in another room within the same little house and as I opened my eyes, I felt him beside me. I looked at him, I looked at my hands where the rope burns were and I asked him, "What have you done? What have you done?" I wanted to cry but I could not.

He turned, smiled as he stroked my cheek.

"Morning baby," he said.

"What did you do?" I asked.

"Here let me show you; it seems you have already forgotten," he replied.

He proceeded to do it again. I was in shock, I was scared and confused. I did not fight him or scream. I was numb and dumb I could not move. I was frozen stiff. A part of me was still asking: "What you have done?" I was not sure if I was alive, dead or dreaming. I thought of the time I saw a man get hit by a car, only for him to get up and keep walking as though nothing had happened. As he got done, I saw the sunlight make its way into the room and I said to myself, "Damn, I am late for work." I was doing the early morning shift from 6 am.

I jumped up, got dressed and ran. I was not running from him. Like the man who got hit by the car, I was running to work, carrying on as though nothing had happened.

As I did, I would see people staring at me and it was as though they knew what I had done or what he had done to me. I particularly recall the feeling of death coming over me especially because I was walking by Chiromo Mortuary. It was a gripping fear that I had done something dreadfully wrong and sinful. I began to run faster this time from him because of what had happened. I had never felt so detached from myself. It was like I was outside my body watching, but not relating to any of it.

I recall not being able to run anymore and I stood trying to catch my breath. I heard this strange sound of thumping, and I looked around to find where it was coming from. I realized it was my knees shaking and knocking together. I could see them; they were mine, but I could not feel them.

I pulled myself together and made it to work. I told my boss how sorry I was.

"You look bad girl, what did you get into last night?" my boss asked.

"Nothing, my car broke down and it was just one big mess," I responded.

It was the truth, the short version of it.

"Well, alright, go get changed and get to work then," he added.

I got to the changing rooms, took off my clothes, and though I only meant to change, I found myself walking to the shower. I took a cold shower hoping it would wake me up from this nightmare, I did that a few times and it started to become clear that I was not dreaming as I started to feel some aches and stings. I showered several times, but I could still smell him, I still felt filthy.

I got into the kitchen, and not long after, the boss called me and told me he had called my dad to pick me up. It was a weekend and he did not need me and it seemed I needed the time out. I felt relieved. I recall trying to call my friend Naziah to tell her what had happened, but I could not. When I heard my dad was at the gate, I knew I had someone I could finally tell.

When I got to the car, my dad was furious. He had to stop what he was doing to come get me and the car that I had abandoned on the side of the road. He expressed how irresponsible he thought I was. That if I had taken proper care of the car, it would not have stalled and that I had inconvenienced him. I told him I was sorry and tried not to cry as it hit me that it was entirely my fault.

But I still did not understand why my punishment was so severe. I should not have been surprised after all. I was never like any other. I had always drawn the attention of men. Something about me that caused men to react in a certain way towards me. It never happened to other girls, just to me so I believed it was me, it was in me, it was my fault.

I met with the guy again, not long after, at a bar and all I could do was walk up to him and ask him for his name. I thought to myself that he was my first and every girl should know who her first was. Even though I would not have the experiences all others did, I was going to have that, his name. I wish I could say that it got better, that I talked about it and did something about it but I did not. I had already concluded that it was my fault and as a result, I began to accept the punishment of the thing that I was that made men act the way they did around me. But even in doing so, something new had been introduced in me.

Hurting people hurt others. He had put in me his hurt, and it was rising in me as well. It was as though he took all that pain and put it in me. I could feel it and almost taste it. It was foul and cruel and every bit as beastly and monstrous as he. It was in me, growing and consuming me and no matter how hard I tried to fight it. This thing seemed to take the wheel and turn my life around. I was swerving out of control. He was my first, but not by far my last.

When one goes through such an incident, the first thing that happens is denial. The trauma and the shock keep the reality of it at bay. We also cannot bring ourselves to believe what happened to us. The next stage is where we start to analyze things asking ourselves why and then begin to blame ourselves. Because we believe it is our fault in some way, we accept the punishment and everything else that happens. I also could not bring myself to tell because of what people would think and do. In most cases, people do not help as much as they destroy. I did not want to be treated like an outcast any more than I had already been treated.

Where does one go from here? The many effects of rape on an individual are so profound that the ones on the outside looking in are quickly led to judge and label you things.

The idea of reporting what had happened, the idea of going to the hospital or police to be examined, to have to tell my story over and over, to have everyone know, to be touched and poked; probed and tested, is one I also could not bear.

I much later came to learn that I did everything wrong, I messed up even more by showering, changing my clothes, combing or washing my hair and all else. The most natural feeling is disgust, filth and shame. The most natural action to take is to clean oneself and yet that is the thing not to do.

A rape victim should go to the hospital to be examined. He or she should neither shower nor change, before seeing a specialist. It's not easy, but it could save your life and that of another by making sure you got treated and tested. It could also ensure that the rapist is caught before he attacks another person.

If it were to happen again, I would follow protocol. Would I feel any less violated? No. Would I be any more comfortable? No. But I would not care so much about my reputation or privacy as I did then. I wish one could wait to heal and recover after rape before they reported it, but it is a matter of urgency. Not so much so they can apprehend the culprit, but also save you any more harm that may come in form of an infection, disease and even pregnancy. At times, any physical harm that may have been caused needs medical attention, too.

I came to realize that when a rapist is caught and put behind bars, we put an end to him raping anyone else. However, that does not solve the issues of rape and why it happens. I believe that many sex offenders and child abusers were in their own way offended and abused. I believe it is something passed on physically, mentally and beyond through exposure and experience of sorts.

I forgive anyone who ever hurt me as a child in this manner. In more ways than one, I can understand the pain and anguish of my abuser and rapist more than any other can. I would call it doing onto others what was done onto you. It is not to punish, to harm but to quench and fill something that is within. I would sit with these people and instead understand where it comes from. The way to solve problems is not to cut their heads off, but to find the root and uproot it from there.

For the rape victim, here is my message for you: It was never your fault. You are not being punished. You may not have had a choice then, but you have a choice now. The choice to rise above and go past it. The best, the only way to heal is to get immediate help, medically, mentally and spiritually. I know you may want to hide, and forget, but something like this only gets bigger and worse with time. Don't do what I did, get help.

Chapter 5
My Drink

After my rape incident, I tried to do what I assume some, as victims of rape, would do. I say victim because until you and I are no longer held captive by the rape, you are a victim. Until you survive it and move past it totally you are still in it. I was not sure if I would survive. I was not doing too well, so I tried to drown it out and began to drink.

I usually had a drink or two, but at this point something happened and I began to drink more than usual. I was still working at the hotel and during breaks, I would go across the road to the bars that I often saw but never walked into. I never had reason to until now. I walked in and ordered a drink. I needed something I could take fast and that would work fast. Something straight to the point that would hit the core of my pain, that part of my mind where the memory of him was and aimed at it like a dart to a dart board. I would go and take shots and when done, go back, get changed and get to work. I was good at what I did, so even under the influence, I did it well. I was even better at hiding my feelings under a smile. I spoke words of joy, but deep down in me, were all the opposite.

I drank because every time I felt the tears and the pain in my throat, I would shoot up this hot drink that would send it all so far away. I wanted to believe that what I went through was a nightmare and the worst imagination ever.

I thought it had to be real because it seemed unimaginable. I drank because, though now I knew it was real, I could not face or accept it. It began across the road on breaks, but moved to the work place. I had made friends with the bar men and now I had access to it all. I would stay after work and drink. I knew what to drink, what to mix and what not to. I became an expert drunk. I was never late to work or clumsy. I spoke clearly and well, I gave no signs. I never shook other than when I was driving home at night or heard a sound in the hour or when I saw a shadow pass by. Yes, I shook but not from my drink but fear.

My drink was my friend and my comfort. It would embrace me, but sooner or later, it would leave and I could not feel it anymore. I needed to keep that feeling with me, and so I took more and more shots; two or three then seven and then a bottle. No day or night would pass without me having a drink. I changed overnight. I was less happy, even though I could get high. I sunk lower than when I took off. Alcohol is a depressant. We take it to get high to run away not knowing that when it drops us we fall harder and go deeper than before, until we are in a bottomless pit.

You look up one day and you are so far down that you can't see the surface. You can't climb out because with each sip you dug a grave. Though it was killing me, the drink allowed me to live through the hell. Alcohol is a poison, I would compare it to bitterness itself. I drank shot after shot of it, bottle after bottle of this poison. Alcohol made me its slave: it was my master. The pain it caused, the marks it left behind were just like the marks of the lashes on a slave's back.

When one goes out into their day to day life sober then suddenly comes home drunk and a different person, parents may say you have rebelled, but a sudden and drastic change in behaviour is not a sign of rebellion but a cry for help. It is a sign that something has gone terribly wrong; that something hit them hard. Something traumatic, tragic that they can't talk about. Something is wrong if you have to drink each day to get by.

Do not look at such people in disgust and disappointment. Look beyond to what they cannot say or do. Look beyond what they smell like, and hear their cry for help. They are looking for something, someone, a way out and they seem to only find that at the bottom of the glass.

When I could not get help, when I could not find a way out, I found myself searching and trying something else. This time I would have my revenge. I would take my perpetrator and bring him where I was now - the bottom of the pit. I was in hell.

Chapter 6
My Bed

I tried to forget my pain. I tried to make the drink a new friend, but it seemed to have turned against me. As I sat at the bar, I could not bring myself to talk about it with others.

I was untouched in a sense. What they had taken from me as a child was bad enough, but I still had that one thing that I believed I had a choice as to whom I would give it to. I had believed that I had a choice as to who would be my first. I had held on and waited this long only to have it taken from me by force.

I recall women talking and saying that that girl had been ruined because she gave herself so loosely to someone out of wedlock. I had not given mine; it had been taken. What I was left with was the same ruin. I had been ruined, defiled, touched, broken and no longer a virgin. It did not matter how it happened just that it did.

Then this thought hit me. They were going to take it from me anyway so why not just give it? It would be less painful and at least I would have some control.

Something happened to awaken the monster my abuser had left in me. I began to do things that I think he would do. I began to sit at the bar and wait for my opportunity to make my kill. I was once the hunted and now I had become the hunter. I was waiting like a lion ready to pounce on its prey. I looked for those who walked tall and talked tough. I knew they were the ones I wanted to break and take back my revenge. I was going to do to them what they did to me. I looked for them. I swung my hips. I licked my lips. I spoke sweet seductive words that lured them into my bed. This was my plan; I would bring them into my bed and slay them.

When they got here, I allowed them to put on a show not knowing that I had become numb to everything they had to offer. I had no feeling or sensation. I felt no pleasure from their kisses and touch. All the pleasure I got was from giving them no reaction. I took to yawning as they did their thing, looking at the ceiling, lighting a smoke and asking them to hurry as I was bored. I took pleasure in making them feel small as they had me.

I knew that men would do things to women, kiss and tell, brag but here I knew they would have nothing to brag about as I was totally unmoved and unshaken. I was dead and no matter what they did, I felt nothing. It was a pleasure to watch the frustration, the wonder and the shame of them not being able to please me. It was a pleasure that put a smile on my face and gave me purpose – to feed on their shame, disappointment and frustration. It elevated me. It was my new high. I felt good, like I had given them a taste of their own medicine.

"I am bored, hurry up, finish and get out," I said to one man.

"What kind of woman are you? Are you a devil that you have no feelings or are you a prostitute that you are so used to lying down with men?" he responded.

Though that was the case, there was a part of me that wanted to take back that moment that I should have enjoyed and taken pleasure in. I wanted to enjoy it as I would and should have if I had chosen and given myself to someone. It was a choice to make. I was trying to get that back. One after the other they came to my bed and one after the other they left me feeling dead. No pain, pleasure, joy or sorrow; just dead. I went out over and over again as the beast in me grew hungry and devoured every man that came and yet no amount of their shame could quench its thirst for revenge. It was a monster that fed off it. And what little pleasure I got from my vengeance! That's the thing about lust and greed, when you go after something to fill your emptiness it is never enough. It could never satisfy you. Pain, tragedy and hurt are not taken away by causing others pain but through love and forgiveness.

When we break, it takes love and care to brace us back together. I was broken and I had to break them. I was in hell and I was going to bring as many of them as I could. As far as I was concerned, men belonged in hell. My bed and my legs were their gateway to it and I welcomed all that would walk my way to it. I never knew one could have so much anger, bitterness and hate and that it would consume you to such a level.

My bed was the stage on which I took my revenge, where I had set up a plot to destroy every man I could. My bed was not a place to lay your head, find rest or comfort. Mine was a place where heads would roll and nightmares would come. I wanted them to die as I had. Though my bed had no blood stains, it was stained with their pain. They say as you make your bed so shall you lie on it. Mine was made of tears and pain that burnt my soul each day I lay in it. And I needed them to burn, too.

Chapter 7
My Girlfriend

I have come to learn that one of the things that may happen to some women who have been sexually assaulted by men is that they turn to same-sex relationships. This is as a result of not healing and the anger they still carry. I have learnt that this is not a solution nor is it acceptable. I do not support or agree with gay or lesbian relationships. As the Bible says, it is an abomination.

I had grown weary of my bed. I had brought all those to my bed and there were no more left. I thought if I could not take revenge and I could not face it, I would run from it. I packed up and moved across the border to Tanzania. I was looking for change. I wanted to start over a new page and write a new story. So I went somewhere. I wanted to find new people, a new name, new house, new environment and even learn a new language to some level. But I was the same old me with the same memories of the same thing happening to me all over again. I still carried the same monster. The farther I ran, the more it gripped me.

It seemed like the thing I was running from was tattooed on my skin. I could not get away from it. It was who I had become. In this new place, something new happened. A combination of all the old things came together into one: my drink and my bed. I began to drink again. I became more active in my bed.

I took it to a whole new level to humiliate men. I was invited to a friend's house where she lived with her boyfriend. Her name was Sally and she sold guns. I liked her because she had gained power as a woman through guns. There was something about holding that cold metallic object that could kill that made me feel powerful. Having a gun could make a man fall on his knees crying and begging. She had found her power and I had found mine and I realised the two combined would be a force to reckon with. That night, her man and I went back to her place. She was attracted to me, to my power and she was drawn to me as she was to her man.

What began as an attraction of the power held by the woman soon degenerated into something else. I decided to take the man's woman away from him to revenge for all the pain men had caused. The monster I had become drove me into a same-sex relationship in order to avenge the bad things men had done to me. As I write these things, I cannot believe just how much of a monster I had become, I was sick, sickening and I don't write it for you to take pleasure, but to understand how far I had gone, how low I had sunk.

What began as pleasure became pain and fuelled my anger more, I did not want to be them and now I was. I was doing to her what they did to me. It broke me that I broke her. It hurt me that I hurt her. It pained me that I pained her and I drove myself to love her as she was not my target. So to undo what I had done, I loved her and was kind to her and gave her all I could.

In the end, that is not who I was. I was not born to be with a woman. It was still not natural to me. Although I had justified all I had done, I knew this was not it. I had turned against my own, in a blind hopeless pursuit to bring the man down. I was bitter and angry with the urge to destroy him.

That was part of the reason I stayed. I was sick of the men. I did not want them around me. Perhaps my own would understand me but that was not how we were designed. I had to leave her and it was by far one of the most painful and hateful things I had done.

"All things come to an end and it's time to end this," I remember saying.

"Why are you saying that? Why are you doing this to me?" Sally replied.

"What did you hope would come of this? Did you think I was going to take you home to my parents? That we were going to get married and have children? How? How can two women make a baby?" I said.

"Please don't say such hurtful things," she said.

"You are a fool for not seeing this coming," I said.

"You are so cruel and cold. Are you the she-devil, he-devil, an animal or what?" she replied.

"That, my dear is by far the greatest compliment I have been paid. But compliments will get you nowhere. We are done, now please leave me alone. Leave, and do not look back. Do not call me or think of me. Go find a man or become a nun, whatever you do just don't do it here," I said.

She did not deserve it. I broke her heart. I had become all the men who had broken me and was doing to her and others as they did to me. It is not men only who had failed her and broken her but I had, too. She gave me a ring that I wore on my toe for all these years and only recently took it off. I carried it in some hope to have her forgiveness and prayed that God would heal her and give her joy instead of sorrow that I had caused. We were both hurt. She got hurt the most and she was not even my target. She was a means to an end and I was mean to her.

I do not know where Sally is, what she is like or if she recovered. If only this book would end up in her hands, she could read how deeply sorry I am for what I did.

I pray that God will touch her, bless her and give her peace. I pray I will meet her at the gates of heaven and know that she made it, and though this is not related to the kind of relationship we had, it is to the one I have with my maker.

Chapter 8
My Music

At this stage in my life, in this new country going through all the things I was going through, and having done what I had done to my girlfriend, I looked at my life and thought to myself that something had to change. I was training in a radio station, not so much a job for me, but being close to something that made me come alive - music. There is something about music that makes everything work. It seems like everything is right when there is music to go with it. I think everybody in life needs a soundtrack. I have a gift that runs through my family and it's a gift of song, music and rhythm. I wanted to venture out and try it as it was the one thing that gave me pleasure.

I remember composing music in high school and I thought I could do this. I got an opportunity to do it with a producer who I had met who offered me an audition in Zanzibar. I flew there and found they already had a beat that needed words and my voice. It was on a Friday when I arrived and we hit the ground running. It was effortless and easy as though it was something I was born to do. In no time, I was done. We recorded that song that same Friday, mixed and mastered on Saturday, and on Sunday, it was sent out. On Monday I was on air and it became a hit. The song was *Nasonga Mbele*.

I later got a call from a man I had been with who asked if it was about him. I have to say it was about every man. I felt like a chick in the claws of an eagle. It was about every man who had abused, beaten, raped me, brought me down, spoke to me words that killed and broke my spirit and altered what I was born to be.

I was awarded a contract shortly after to record an entire album. It was the first time in a long time I was excited about life. I would come to the studio for a week and create music, record and have a great time. Everything was going great until that one night when my producer, Salim, looked at me with a look I knew. It warned me of the danger that was to come. A look that told me to run but to where?

As we were shutting down the studio, he called me to his room. This was not unusual, as we would usually do this as we went over the programme for the following day. But I sensed something was different. He reached out and grabbed me. It was with such a forceful hate and lust. I pulled back but he pulled me in again and ripped my shirt. He did not even realize he had. He was burning with desire.

Salim then hit me so hard that I did not realize when he took the rest of my clothes off. In shaky voice, I begged him to stop. In my head, I was screaming but when I opened my mouth to speak it was a whisper. I did not know what to think or do and it was all happening so fast. I realized for the first time that I could actually die. I had encountered a beast. A beast had no issue getting what it wanted dead or alive.

"Salim please! Please stop! Someone help me," I cried.

"You have to do better than that. Can't you scream or shout? And I promise you if you try I will kill you and still have my way with you," he responded.

He said this as he had his hand around my neck squeezing, allowing me to breathe just barely. I knew he was serious and I did not dare to make a sound I think I even held my breath, afraid he or someone would hear me breathing. Tears run down my face, but even they knew not to make a sound as they hit the floor.

I had to stay on for another week or so and this continued every night. The studio was in a secluded place and I was still not so familiar with the route. I also needed my passport which he had for safe keeping. I was trapped. I turned to what I knew how to do. I would wake up and have black coffee, but in place of water I would use vodka. I would also smoke. I was scared, but I had to perform because if I did not, he said he would kill me. I had to perform on stage and in his room, and I did.

This was my survival and each night I would tell myself I would not fight him, but each night when I saw him, I did and he beat me. I do not recall every time, but I do recall the night he came into my room and I looked at him and he knew I was going to fight. He tried to tell me to co-operate, he even asked me to pretend for that one night that I actually liked it. Pretend that I loved him. I knew then what he felt. He, like me, was looking for love. He was looking for someone who could love him for him and when this did not happen, he took it by force. Part of me hurt for him but the rest of me screamed for myself and I spat in his face and at his words.

At that moment, I knew to brace myself for anything. I believed after what I had just done, I would never see the morning. He hit me so hard that I flew across the room, hit my head on the wardrobe, and on the floor. Before I could figure out what was happening, he grabbed my leg and pulled me towards him. He hit me again as he took off his belt. He proceeded to rape me. This time his aim was not to get pleasure from being with me but from hurting me. He had such rage and bitterness and he used all that as he raped me on the floor. I am not sure which hurt more; him ripping my insides or the carpet burning the skin on my back. With each move, it felt like the skin was being peeled off my back. I hoped when he was done he would kill me.

He stayed away from my face and hands parts of my body that were visible or before people. So he knew how to break a woman and hide it. He bought me a bottle every day and introduced me to hashish. He was willing to give me these things as he was not willing to stop and let me go.

I was in a contract with the devil; one I could not buy myself out of. When I went to the main land and stayed too long, he would send people to come get me. He owned me, I was his slave. At the time, I was seeing a man named Max and another man and he knew it.

Allow me to detour a bit and share a little about Max. I met Max at a concert. He seemed fun and interesting and we seemed to have a few things in common seeing as he had lived in Kenya for a while. I also knew and schooled with his brother and cousins back in high school, which I found out as we got to know each other.

It was not anything in particular about Max that made me give him a chance. He was another guy that I met and chose to see. In fact, I have to confess I was not always faithful to him. My relationships had nothing to do with love or real feelings of affection but the effect of the pain and hurt I had gone though.

Max happened to be the one I liked most; the one who also actually treated me like a girlfriend and not just a sex object so I gave that a chance.

My producer, Salim, knew I was seeing Max. He would beat me for being with another man and being cheap as he called me.

"You are a whore! You are a filthy whore. You dare to have any other man but me?" Salim asked.

"I am not a whore, and I am not your woman I will never be yours," I responded.

"You foolish woman, don't you know I could kill you?" Salim continued.

I took his hand and put it around my neck.

"Please, please Salim, kill me, I would rather be dead than be with you," I begged.

"You are a foolish woman, but I can't lose you. I have invested too much. Get to the studio, we have work to do," he said.

I was losing my mind. All in all, my music helped me get by. I would go in and just sing. I would go in and just get lost in the beats. With music, nothing could touch me; nothing hurt. I got done with the album and I was glad. I began to get sick. I would see the doctors and they would tell me I had malaria, test after test. I had lost so much weight. I thought I had HIV. All I could think of was that God could at least give me a better way to die.

As time passed, Salim got weary of me and since he got what he wanted, he was okay with letting me go. Though I recall those words he spoke to me, "If you are going to die, then go die at home, not here."

I went back home and made an appointment with a doctor. I was so surprised as what I thought was death in me was actually life. Even though I had lost my life and voice and my music to that man, I knew I had gained something else.

It's not always easy to move on from our past. In my case, I have never stepped back into a studio since then or sang before people. I always said that the devil stole my voice. Though I sing in church or in the shower, this is one place that I know God is yet to restore me and crown me.

In my rage, I looked at Salim just before I left for the last time and spoke words that I lived to regret. I looked at him and said, "I wish you drop dead." I never thought about those words again till recently when I was chatting online with a mutual friend called Feisal. He told me that Salim came to Nairobi and while there, he just dropped dead. I could not believe it untill I got online and looked it up. He was in Nairobi on business when he just collapsed and died. Investigations were inconclusive as to what killed him.

"Feisal, I never told you this, but Salim would rape me and beat me. I could not tell anyone and I was so scared," I said.

"I am so sorry. Is that why you left and never came back? How could you live with it all this time?" he responded.

"How could I have reported what had happened? Who would have believed me? The last thing I told him was to drop dead and now you tell me he did. Feisal, did I kill him?" I asked.

"Never think that, he did terrible things and you said terrible things, but you are not responsible for his death. All that are living must one day die. It's not your fault," Feisal responded.

I was gripped with fear as I recalled what I had told him. The words I spoke had come to pass and now I knew better the power of words, but I had forgotten the ones I had once spoken. The Bible says, 'speak life'; that the tongue has the power of life and death and I knew it now to be all too true. Death heard me and it fulfilled my command.

Even in your deepest anger, don't open your mouth to speak death events to they that you feel deserve it. There is no pleasure or satisfaction when it actually happens. As strange as this may seem, it broke me and I grieved and mourned for Salim. Regardless of what he had done, I was not the same girl anymore. I had forgiven him and I was saddened by the loss of a life. I understood that there was something more to what he did than most people would think. I am not making excuses for abusers and rapists. I am just saying that there is something that leads them to act and they, like their victims, need help. They, like their victims, are suffering.

Understand that what's done is done, even if the person is in jail and dead it will never change the past. The best way to move on and get your life back is to forgive.

I want to say to Salim, that I forgive him for all he ever did – and I pray that in his final moments, he chose Christ.

Forgiveness does not mean they are right and you are wrong. It just means it happened; there was hurt and that you are willing and ready to heal and move on. Forgiveness is not tolerating the deed, just not letting it take over your life any more than it already has. Letting go and letting God deal with the other person.

Chapter 9
My Baby

I had returned to Kenya because I was really sick and I thought I was going to die from the lifestyle I had lived. I would have liked to die at home. I was not coming home for chit chat. I was just coming to rest and die. As I mentioned earlier, what I thought was death was actually life.

They sent me to have an ultra sound scan. The results were evident. I was pregnant and going into my second trimester.

I don't know how all the others missed it. Maybe it was the drugs and alcohol. Maybe it was God hiding it so that Salim would not find out and beat it out of me. I was happy because I was not dying; instead I was living. We were living. I thought to myself how it was when I deserved death I got life. I recall trying to tell my dad, but he was busy and so I wrote him a letter. He called me and asked me if I wanted to raise the child as my own or allow him to adopt and raise the child as his and I would always have a relationship with my baby.

There is something about my dad; he has a way of being there and he is great. I looked at him with tears rolling down my face when he said that he would accept my decision. He told me that he would do everything to have us both healthy and that all would be fine.

"Things happen, but how we react can make it better or worse. Mum and I can adopt your child as our own if you like," said dad.

"This is my doing, my responsibility, my baby. I will raise it as my own. Thank you, baba," I responded.

"I respect that, and we will do it all together. Would you like me to tell your mum?" he said.

"Yes please. I can't tell mum," I pleaded.

"Alright, go get something to eat and rest. I know this is overwhelming. It will be alright. You are not alone. Thank you for trusting me with this," he said.

I was pregnant. I knew who the baby belonged to. Salim would never touch me without protection. He called me a filthy whore and I knew it was not his. I was glad that at the very least, as he raped me he was kind enough to use protection. I know it was more for his own protection than mine. It is ironic though, if he could not stand me, why did he want me? I knew my boyfriend, Max, was responsible for the pregnancy.

I recall being on the phone with him.

"I went to the doctor and they know what's wrong with me. I am pregnant."

"Jesus Christ," he said.

I am not sure what I was supposed to think after that. He said it as though he had just made the biggest mistake of his life. I knew right then that this would be my baby and I would be in it alone and could not rely or depend on him. I did not care because I had been given life in place of death and I was going to take this opportunity to make the best of it.

My baby was something else. I remember him moving in me, kicking, dancing to music. He loved the pool and the gym and I did 60 laps a day and it seemed to put him to sleep.

My baby was my gift and I was not going to let anything spoil that. I was determined to enjoy it. I called my old friend Naziah and she was with me through and through. She was a great help to me. She is still a good friend to date. I did everything I could do to get healthy and gain weight for the baby and myself.

I recall the meeting with my folks and Max. I recall the way he said he did not want to marry me. It was as though it was a ridiculous question, but in my head, I could not think of anything worse than tying myself to a man till death do us part. I knew then more than ever that a man would have to kill me or I kill him if we were married. Death was definitely going to do us part.

"It is my baby, and I will take responsibility, but I do not want to get married," Max said.

"I do not want to get married either. Two wrongs don't make a right. Marrying him is not the way to deal with or fix what we did," I replied.

I had a hard time gaining weight as I was very underweight. I was drinking, smoking and on drugs in my first trimester. I recall praying, something I had never done before. I prayed to have a boy. I still had my reservations about life as a girl. I believed being born a boy was better. I then prayed that God would make my baby healthy and keep the baby from what I had done.

While I was pregnant, I ate a lot of cheese which was unusual. Today I look at my son and how he gobbles up cheese and I laugh. Every time my brother spoke near me or to me, my baby would kick and today my son hears my brothers voice and jumps up in joy to go greet him. I could not believe that I had such love for something that I had never seen or held. I questioned that love existed or that I was capable of giving or receiving it and yet here I was. It was the most interesting experience of my life. I had come from a place of nothing to live for, to having something so precious that I loved with magnitude. I could not see how people called babies unwanted or a mistake.

Although I had grown so angry and bitter, this baby was softening me in ways I could not comprehend. Even though I was going through Max's rejection, I was in awe of everything that was happening to me. Even with my body, it felt like for the first time, this body I had, had fulfilled a purpose. It was finally of more value than just a sexual object. I was a vessel to bring a life. Each day, my body changed and transformed to something beautiful and amazing. It effortlessly made room and adjusted to the need of my baby and it amazed me. Something about being pregnant made me understand the level to which God could care for His children. The woman's body is made to hold, care and protect this living being that had miraculously come to be.

I realised then that it could never be a mistake. Getting pregnant even in sin could never be a mistake. I had been created and put in my mother's womb – a place that is designed to hold that life.

My baby boy was born on the 20th February 2004 on a Friday at 12:27 am. He weighed 3.5kgs and I had never seen anything like him. He did not look all cute and cuddly like they do in movies. He was wrinkled and his complexion was one I did not recognise. I had what they call a blue baby.

I had felt so useful with him in me. I felt life and now he was out, he did not need me and I could not feel the life in me. To make things worse, I was not able to breastfeed him. I have never felt so useless.

With the help of my family, my mum and her friends I was able to get by and soon began breastfeeding. I grew to love being a mum. After a few days, my baby looked more like the babies I was used to seeing. He was so tiny and adorable and everyone loved him.

We called him Sholinke Kariba Munio. Sholinke is a Masaai name given in honour of my grandmother who was Masaai and the rest are my father's names.

It feels great to be Shobe's mother. I love this gift of a child. I believe God has given me all I need to be his mum. I will fight for him, love him, and stand by him in love always. I will strive to be the best mum I can be not just to him, but to all children and the ones I'm yet to have.

Chapter 10
My Mind

I have met many people in life. I have had both friends, and enemies. I have had family and I have had those that are neither here nor there. Out of all the people I met and interacted with, I came to realise that I was my very own worst enemy.

As a child, there were some cartoons we watched in which there would be a character in a dilemma. He would appear as himself in the form of an angel on one shoulder, giving him all sorts of good advice and in the form of the devil on the other shoulder giving him bad advice. It was entertaining and I loved it.

Whoever did the cartoon captured what really goes on in our minds. I felt like there were two voices in my head; one pointing me in the right direction and the other leading me to all manner of vices.

I really cannot say or recall when they came to be. Only that over time, it seemed like one had moved out or maybe the other one had buried her somewhere in the depths of my mind because I could not hear her any more. She was never there to give me all the good advice she used to before. I guess I was a disappointment even to my own voice of reason. What I did not know at the time, that I now know, is that I had schizophrenia. I was different people at different points of my life. Walk with me as I uncover who they were.

In various stages of my life, I had different names. As I look back at that now, I see that each of these were the different people I had grown to be and still carried with me as I went along life's journey.

Botu

As a child, they nicknamed me Botu, a sweet little girl; strong, outspoken with an iron-clad will. I loved the outdoors, loved flowers and loved life. Life, however, did not love me back, and even at such an early stage, it had allowed the beasts of this world to devour my innocence.

My childhood seemed ever so short-lived. One day I was learning how to spell, the next I was discovering parts of my body I never knew I had, let alone being forced to see the male anatomy.

I came to learn that men, and the little boys I played with in school, were two completely different creatures. I did not believe one grew up to be the other.

June

I then became my most despised companion or personality of all times, June. To this day, I cannot say her name and hear it without feeling some form of hatred towards her. June tried too hard to make everyone happy and make everyone love her even when she knew they never would. She was weak and desperate and if she could have just grown some skin, we would never have been in the mess we found ourselves in.

June loved and adored her father, but it seemed she was quickly losing his affection by not being all that he hoped for. Grades meant everything to him and as long as they were up so was his love and affection, but June was on a low and there was just too much going on around her to get them back up. Though she never got the affection she may have wanted from her dad, it seemed that other men were not shy of giving it to her, only it was not fatherly love.

I hated June's mum. I hated the way she yelled her name and I still do. Part of me also hated her mum because I feel like since her dad was gone most of the time she was meant to be watching me and yet all these things happened. Could she not see it? How could she let this happen? Where was she?

Didn't she ever suspect something was not right? I mean, I was sick; I would burn when I peed. Was she blind, or in denial? It was hard enough not having dad around and now I had to deal with a mother who I do not know where she was. It was too hard to hate dad, I loved him, but I hated him for being absent.

I recall my mother and father telling stories of how I would fall ill every time my father would travel. That alone should have raised a red flag in my parents. If that happens, clearly the condition is far more than a cold. There is something about the separation from the father that made this child ill and that should not have been brushed aside as though it was something the child did because she missed her father so much. As I look back now, I can see that the psychological issue began there and that could have been arrested and dealt with at that stage.

As I grew older, I began to change. I also had to change my name and grow out of my baby name. I was June Muniu. I could not help what had happened to me as a child, but I was going to help what happened to me in primary and high school. I was a beautiful child; I knew that because many men told me that. I also knew that because I found myself on display as a flower girl at every wedding in the family. I began to draw lines between my looks and how I was treated and saw the connection.

When I was in class 7, I had just passed my entrance exam to Form One and to cross over from the 8-4-4 system to the British system. One evening at the end of the school day, one of my friends came over to me and said that he had a friend who wanted to meet me and say hi. I assumed it was one of the kids from some other class that I did not know so I agreed to meet him. As the guy approached I realised that my assumption was way off, the guy was in high school! He came over and said hi looking at me as he licked his lips. I thought this was very bizarre. I recall him introducing himself and inviting me somewhere, as he welcomed me to high school.

He could have left it at that but he did not. He stepped closer to me, and he leaned over as though he was going to kiss me on the cheek, but instead he took in a deep whiff of my hair, rubbed it between his fingers and told me that I had beautiful hair. Any time a man said that anything about me was beautiful, I knew I was in danger. There was something about him smelling my hair that just made my stomach churn. It brought back the feeling I had with the gardener and I hated it. I stayed cool, but inside, I was running wild screaming for my daddy.

When I got home that day, I went and got a pair of scissors and began to cut my hair. My mum and her friend were around and I asked them to help me cut my long beautiful hair, and they did. I then took on a new personality. I wore boy clothes and did boyish things and prayed and wished God would make me one so that boys would not notice me and do things to me as they wanted to do with girls. This move put me right into the weird girls' box in school, I was that tomboy and that was not a very popular thing to be.

June tried hard to stay out of the radar and carry on as if she was not a girl. As puberty struck, it was interesting that I believed so much I was a boy that my breasts hardly grew. Others laughed, I got teased a lot, but I never got noticed and I was glad. I was often told I had beautiful legs and I had to take care of that too.

As a member of the swimming team, I would get some joint problems now and then. The doctor advised me to cover up and stay warm since where our school was located would get rather chilly. I got permission to wear trousers in school and I was going to make sure that I never had to wear a skirt again and show my legs. I found myself getting caught up in so-called love affairs in school. I did this to appear normal, but most times, I just had friends that were boys and that did not go down well with their girlfriends.

High school was terrible. I was not good at Math. What I was good and great at were not considered real subjects or anything one could make a real career out of. I swam, played basketball, loved music and art. In French class, the only thing I ever learnt was the insulting things my teacher tossed. 'That is not correct' and 'you are stupid' in French is as much as I can say. In Math class, I had no idea what the teacher was teaching or if he was teaching at all or just talking in numeric as another language. In English, I was like a peasant in spelling, my grammar was horrifying. I felt like an alien on earth only without superpowers.

We were nearing the end of high school and this was a great time to change into someone new. June had succeeded at being a tomboy, but she was stupid and had no skills. She was going to fail. She had learnt nothing other than hating the teachers as much as she hated herself. They asked us what names we wanted to register with in our final exams and this was her chance. The name changed from June Muniu to Thitu Kariba.

Thitu

The thing about change is that it cannot only take place on the outside. Many times we think we can change our looks, our clothes, our names or even where we live and that will make the difference, but it does not.

I was a mess. I had no belief in God. I believed He existed but I was certain I was not His type. I was not smart, I was not a good girl like the ones in Christian Union, and I was not even sure I was meant to be a girl. I had too much going on and it was clear at the time that God had his hands full with useful and worthy people. If anyone was nice to me, it was because they wanted something from me and most time they did not even ask but just took it.

V2

I acquired a nick name V2 which came from 'Vituko' which is Swahili for drama. I was full of drama. I was on table tops dancing, making out in the car, smoking and getting high on the beach. I was skinny dipping in the ocean and pools. To this day I say it is as though the man who raped me put something in me. I remember how I used to also say that the name V2 also stood for Venom, but in my case, it was as though it had multiplied. I was twice as bad as he was.

V2 came back home pregnant and battered by man and substances. I was Thitu by day and V2 by night. Until now as I write this I had never seen the many pieces that I had been broken into. Eventually, I got a job in one of the media houses and was Thitu again on most days but V2 had her way now and then.

V2 was uncontrollable; she flirted with the CEO at the office, went out drinking and even doing drugs with some work mates. It was not that I did not care but it's like I had no control over me. Both Thitu and V2 were strong personalities and it was a battle. V2 had realised that it was time to eat or be eaten and she became a monster.

My constant and deadly companion

One day as I went about duties at a media house where I worked, I passed out suddenly. The doctors said it was a panic attack. That began a whole new life for me. It was not exactly the kind of change I was going for. There was so much happening around me, so many voices and so much noise. Doctors were saying this, my parents saying that, my boss saying another and from nowhere, there was a voice I had never heard before. The voice had no name, and it seemed to pick up every face in the crowd. It silenced every voice around me.

"They are right you know, you are losing your mind, not that you had much of a mind to lose – you were not the brightest student," the voice would say.

"Did you see how your father looked at you? Poor man, his only daughter and she turned out to be you!"

I was not sure what was real anymore and what was not but I believed that this voice was the only one that told me the truth about all the things I had gone through. I did not know what I hated more; the noise others brought or the one in the head? At times I liked the voice; at least it did not lie to me, but other times I hated it for constantly telling me how messed up I was.

The voice had a great memory. It had recorded and stored every bad thing anyone ever said to me. It kept me awake at night. We would go over list after list of my worthlessness and why killing myself would be the best gift I could give to anyone if I loved them. I was diagnosed with depression, schizophrenia and now I had insomnia.

Each doctor's visit got me new drugs for a new condition. I loved sleeping. It was the only time the voices and noises would shut up; but it would have to be drug induced sleep. Sleeping pills became my best friend.

The cutter

To function, I had to talk myself out of what the voice was saying. I had to talk back at him and shut him up. Unfortunately, while he was in my head where no one could see or hear him, I spoke to him out loud. Today, I see mad men or women walking around pulling their hair and talking to themselves and I totally understand.

I loved pain. I became addicted to pain. It was the only thing left that I could feel. The thing about joy and happiness is that it cannot be inflicted on you physically. It takes mental impact to create positive feelings and yes, bad ones too, but pain is the only thing you can induce physically. Unlike drugs or alcohol, it costs nothing.

I began by using my shaving razors to make small clean shallow cuts on my wrists. It felt amazing. There were pains deep inside of me. It almost felt like when the blood ran down my wrist into the sink, the pain was somehow coming out of me and being washed down the drain.

When I would have my panic attacks, it would feel as though I was trapped in a car, moving at high speed heading right for a concrete wall. I would break into sweat, go paralyzed with fear and could not breathe. The best way to get myself out of this and pull myself back into reality was a jolt that I discovered could be accomplished with sharp pain. Pain became my first aid and I took my razors with me everywhere. I had a case full of them. I had become a cutter. It is a condition where one takes to cutting themselves instead of dealing with the internal pain and issues they are having. I believe it comes about from having repressed too much.

I never wanted to kill myself, I wanted to feel some pain. It sent some adrenaline through my body and brought back some feeling to my life. Cutters know just how deep to go. They may make long, shallow cuts, both on their arms and legs. They are not looking for death, they are not suicidal and I was not, but it was a new addiction.

My doctor was aware of the cutting. However, he was also aware that there was not much they could do beyond psychiatric help. Mental conditions are very difficult to deal with as one cannot operate and cut out the thing causing the problem. I was not locked up, so even if they took my blades, I would just get others. Instead, what they offered me was clean and sanitary blades as I got help so that I would not catch an infection as I did what I did. I am glad they understood and did not try to force change. If a cutter does not get a blade to use, they can use anything that will make a cut. It is like needles to a drug addict and it must be seen and dealt with in the same way. You cannot force the addict to change. You must deal with the underlying issue.

Some of the ways you can identify a cutter is in the way they dress. Since they cut along their hands and wrists and legs, they will wear clothing that covers their scars. They will wear long sleeves, trousers and never want to expose themselves and avoid activities like swimming. A cutter will wear full clothing even in the hottest weather. I would wear my long sleeved sweaters when it was hot. They tend to tag or hold on to their sleeves constantly to keep them from riding up. Cutters could disappear often into the bathrooms and take longer than usual. They may leave bloody tissues around and usually give the excuse that it was a nose bleed. They may carry around a case with them that they never open in front of others and are protective over where they keep their cutting tools. Initially, it may be small cuts on their wrists that you will see and they could give a valid excuse for. As they make more cuts and cover more of the arms or legs they just cover up.

Cutters do not talk or express themselves much. They seem indifferent, and hardly show any emotion. Shortly after an argument or confrontation, they will enter the bathroom or wherever they can go to cut. If you notice these patterns, it could be signs of a cutter. If you confirm this to be so, get help immediately.

One person who helped me greatly when I had my panic attacks was my friend Sonia.

I do not recall what year it was that Sonia and I met, but I do remember how. I had taken my friend to a job interview and I wound up getting the call back. I had not gone for the job, I was not even prepared and yet they found something in me that they liked and wanted. Sonia was already working there as a team leader and I began work immediately. A friendship struck. Sonia would become one of my strong pillars I could lean on.

In my cutting season, Sonia would speak to me and ask me to focus on her voice. She would then insist that I follow her breathing instructions and that would calm me down and get me out of them. I came to learn that God is never far, but always right there and He was there with me through this friend. It is crucial that one person at least always has your back.

I went deeper and deeper in losing my mind as I got more drugs and treatment. I needed out. When you go mad, you not only lose your mind but you also lose everything: your job, your friends, your family, your weight, your dignity, respect and humanity. Doctors do not go behind closed doors to discuss you anymore like a real person. They talk about you right there and as though you were a thing. You are not called by your name but by your patient number, room number or bed number. It takes pain, physical pain to reconnect with the world again, to feel something that confirms that you are still human.

Electric Current Treatment (ECT)

June was nowhere. Thitu was barely holding on and I had no memory at all of Botu.

Things had become so bad that I would spend weeks in institutions and go through electric current treatment. I had completely stopped being human. During the procedure, I recall how they would fasten wires onto my head and give me a mouth guard when they remembered to, so that I could not bite my tongue or cheeks.

ECT erased my memory; I lost everything. It was so bad that if you had come to see me and returned the following day, I would ask you where you had been for so long. I would have completely forgotten the day before. Although it was a means to ease the traumatic memories, it also took my good ones, the ones that consoled me during nights when I could not sleep and wanted to recall what it was like to be human.

Right under your nose

Something about me still reacts to certain smells, and certain smells sometimes trigger a memory recall immediately and other times much later.

We all have things we want to forget but we cannot. We need to deal with them, learn from them and walk away knowing it no longer has a hold on us. The prescription drugs, the ECT, all of that only tried to control and suppress the issue. What I now understand is that I was having a spiritual battle in the physical and it was all happening in my soul. The soul is the contact point between the spiritual and physical, the mind, the emotions and the memories. I still do not think I have a word to explain it all.

Many friends, family, teachers and parents may look at my external traits and call it rebellion. Doctors call it all manner of things but when you take yourself out of the equation, when you stop making it all about yourself, you begin to see the other person screaming out for help.

By the time ECT had come into play, my parents had concluded that I was just looking for attention. They missed the signals years ago and now I was just fighting for my life and I did not care who was looking. Many parents, family members and others at this point come in and try to help. When nothing works to the degree they expect you to, they wash their hands off you. Parents, you cannot come in when a person is in ICU and try to demand they get up and get well. They went through many stages before they got critical. You were probably too busy, or too frustrated, to notice.

It takes a village to raise a child. We all have a part to play in looking out for each other.

No parent wants to be told that their child is ill and more so an illness that you cannot do anything about. Mental illness is something we seem to be ashamed of. It's not imaginary. It's not contagious; it's not witchcraft – it is real. It is not something to sweep under the carpet and not talk about, treating the person like they should be hidden in a dungeon somewhere. This only adds fuel to the fire. That is how they got there to begin with, hiding issues and not talking about them. Mental illness is not permanent and most times it's only a matter of communication, acceptance, forgiveness and love.

I am not ashamed of my mental condition. The more I tried to act normal, the worse it got. I tried for my parents, for my friends and for everyone. But being someone I was not was driving me insane.

Chapter 11
My Doctor

I recall the days when I would lie in my hospital bed waiting for a visitor. It was not that I cared so much about having friends around me. As long as people kept coming, it showed me that even with my condition, I was still seen as a person. There is something about being locked up in a rubber room with no windows, or in a psychiatric ward that no longer qualifies you as a human being but as something that used to be human but malfunctioned. I guess at that point, you realize that being human was not about having a body and a spirit, but having a sound mind.

Each day the doctors and nurses would come and go. Everyone with their own agenda related to my condition but not to me as a person. I was on one drug after the other and as much as I felt better when on them, they kept me from myself. With each dose, with each new treatment, I got further and further away from myself and became just a patient. The ECT life for me got even worse because now I had to have someone else tell me about myself. Sonia, my best friend at the time, would recount what I did or who had come to visit me the day before. I needed more than anything to feel alive. I tried and held on to anything that would give me a moment of that.

Cigarettes helped pass time and give me a slight buzz. To be honest, I think it was just the one thing I had that still felt normal. I hardly ate because the drugs and ECT made my tongue feel nasty and I could not taste anything. Besides, the only appetite I had was for a sense of humanity which I would not find in hospital food.

The chef was great and he came by daily to see if there was something he could make for me. I loved cake and custard, for one it was sweet and I could taste. My mum used to make it for us as kids and it was comforting. I weighed 45kg, smoked 40 cigarettes a day; did not sleep at night, heard voices in my head and was a cutter and that's just to name a few things. It was not long before I heard rumours that people thought I was infected with HIV and with that, came the dropping off of some so-called friends. The best thing about my condition was that even if you said something to hurt me today, chances are I would not remember it the following day.

I do not recall how this all began but, each day a certain doctor would come by my room. He would check on me and we would chat a while in between his busy hospital life. He was a doctor, but he was also a smoker. When I ran out of cigarettes he would share his and when it was time for a smoking break he would have it with me. For the first time in a long time, someone saw me and talked to me. People were not talking to me but about me and around me, deliberating on my case, talking at my condition or ignoring me all together. This particular doctor came to see me and not because he had to, not to serve me in any way as a patient, but because I was a person and he liked me.

It was amazing how patient he was. If I asked things over again the next day, or had an old conversation as though it was new because I could not remember and most of all when I had my panic attacks he never freaked out or looked at me strangely. He simply held my hand, rubbed my back and talked to me. The only other person to do that in all the time when I was ill was my best friend Sonia.

One night as he was coming by to say good night, I asked him for something and he gave it to me. I asked him for a kiss. Many may wonder why I would do that, but when you have lost everything you begin to take inventory of what little you have left. I needed to know if I was still beautiful and desirable. He kissed me and it had an effect on me! It was incredible; I had not felt anything in a long time.

That one kiss felt like a new breath of life. It told me I was alive, I was a woman; desirable and beautiful. I was still worthy of his affection and time. I cannot put in words what that meant to me.

Unfortunately, it did not end with a kiss. Although the kiss had that effect on me, it had another on him and he hinted that he had the key to the room and could lock it for us to have more privacy in case any nurse tried to come in. I know that we had sex, but I have no recollection of it. I would tell Sonia everything while it was still fresh in my mind because I knew that there were chances that I would not remember it. To this day, that story is best told by her and all I do is sit and listen in disbelief.

It was the beginning of my new drug and a relationship. It may have been the first time for me to have made love in my hospital bed, but it was not the last. All in all what we were doing never really hit me. All I knew is that I was alive and human again. Although I knew that I did not love him, I did love how he made me feel.

The relationship continued even after I left the hospital. He understood me. How could he not yet he was a doctor and he knew my condition? He was the closest thing to normal that I had. I may have been the crazy girl, I may have been called or labelled many things, but the one thing about my life that was normal was being in a relationship. Everything else about me made it clear, I was not normal.

The strange part about all this was that it was men who drove me to where I was to begin with, and it was trying to be normal that got me to my breaking point and yet here I was needing a man to make me feel normal. I guess, looking at it now, I was still more crazy than normal and I guess it would take a crazy person to be with me in my condition. I guess being smart, brilliant and a doctor does not make you any more normal than your patients. I suppose we are all crazy and are all looking for some normalcy, some peace and acceptance.

My parents thought I was faking this thing and I know they wished I could just snap out of it. I remember going for counselling sessions with my parents. I could tell they were only present because they had to not because they wanted to. I recall a time when mum had travelled to the States, I was institutionalized again. My father asked us to keep it from her so that it would not ruin her trip. At that point, I felt like an inconvenience, something that ruins people's trips, days and lives.

It is not hard to see why I was drawn to the godless doctor who, clearly had no morals or professional ethics, but was good enough in bed to keep my mind distracted from the hell that I was living in. My relationship with the doctor was not great, but it did get me high.

Unfortunately, it had everything to do with how many drugs I was on. They say that the largest sexual organ is the brain. I was under the influence of drugs that affected this particular organ and helped enhance certain things and feelings that I got when I was with the doctor.

As a result, I found myself needing the doctor just like I did my pills. A person can switch from one addiction to another just as I did. I could stop cutting because I found something or someone else. One can get addicted to food, things, people, anything that will give them the feeling they are looking for. In order to deal with any addiction, we must deal with the why and not the what. Why one starts taking drugs, alcohol, etc., is more important than what they are addicted to. Once one finds the root cause of problems and fills that gap, then they have no need to fill it with substances.

As the relationship carried on, the doctor organised for me to get on board the family planning wagon which I did. I had to use the coil because nothing else worked for me at the time. Not long after that, I got an infection that led to me having to take the coil out for the risk of damaging my tubes. I did this and went on with the pills. I also suggested using protection which did not always go down well with the doctor. We had both been tested for HIV so I was not worried about that. He would be in charge of getting me the pills I needed but often forgot and as you can imagine one thing led to another. I got pregnant.

I recall the day I had to break the news. He began to ask me questions like a patient. He asked when my last period was, whether I was on the pill and Lord knows what else as he cursed passionately. He told me that he was not ready to be a father and that basically even if he were ready I was not the woman he would choose to mother his children. It felt like an out of body experience. I had been down this road before so I really had no expectations. I was already a mum and that was something I held dear. I loved my son and loved children.

"How are you feeling?" he asked.

"Scared and excited all in one," I replied.

"Excited? About what? This is a disaster. We will take care of it," the doctor concluded.

"You mean abort? This is our child," I replied.

"It is not a child, it is just a bunch of cells," he said.

"You say it like is cancer or something to just go in and cut out. I am not having an abortion," I responded.

"Don't be stupid. How are you going to take care of a child, in your condition? Think of what's best for everyone. I'll make arrangements," he reported.

The doctor and I really had nothing much to discuss from then on. He made it clear that he wanted the bunch of cells flushed out before it was too late. I ignored him. And how dare he to ask me questions like he did? I was not a stranger or a patient, I was the woman he had been sleeping with, the one he refused to use protection with and the same one whose pills he often forgot. I already had a dead beat baby daddy so I knew the drill. I knew the silence that would come thereafter and the change in the relationship that was to come. I was having a hard time with him, but even more, I was having a hard time with the pregnancy. I was in pain often and spotted now and then. The sad thing was that it felt as though even my baby did not want me and that hurt more than anything else.

Eventually I broke the news to my parents and their reaction surprised me. They are both saved, and they were deacons of the church and yet they insisted on an abortion.

My parents were not always religious. Growing up they drunk and held many parties and I recall a few not-so-Christian words coming out of my father's mouth aimed at other drivers on the road. Their conversion into Christianity happened later.

I was shocked by their reaction; it changed my perception about them as parents and Christians. I laughed because it felt like I had caught them in a lie. They were just as bad as I and everyone else. I was relieved at how imperfect and hypocritical they were. I suppose to this day, part of me takes delight at knowing every time they criticize me that they are just as human as me. My mother did say something that changed me. She thought that somehow I had planned it all and asked if I really thought a doctor could marry someone like me. It said a lot without saying much and coming from the woman who gave birth to you, you begin to see yourself differently.

If we did not look so alike, I would have been sure I was switched at birth or left at their door step. Given the ultimatums they gave me to kick out the unborn child yet still unwell and the doctor threatening to bail on me; the pressure was mounting and I had a decision to make. My brothers did not know and I was not to tell them... More secrets! No wonder I was crazy! The only person who held on to me was Sonia. Although a saved Christian, she never once judged me or turned away. With each curve ball tossed my way, she loved me more.

Chapter 12
My Angel

Many people have an opinion on abortion and on the people who procure it. The same people have their views about girls who get pregnant out of wedlock. This is not about what is right or what is wrong, this is about the choices we make and how they either imprison us or set us free. I can speak for both sides of the coin. I am both a mother who chose to have an abortion and a mum who had a child out of wedlock.

I knew I was pregnant before the test confirmed it. I was not having morning sickness or anything but I could feel it. I have to say that a part of me was really excited. I felt useful again. I had lost everything and now I was pregnant. I had something and something more precious than a job, friends and the things I had lost. To some extent, I felt alive again though it was short-lived. As soon as I broke the news to the doctor and eventually my folks, the air reeked of death.

With my pregnancy and my already existing condition, my choice became more and more clear, but not at all easier to make.

I waited to the very last minute and then the doctor took me to a hospital where he had arranged and paid for everything. In his definition of the word, he was being a total gentleman. Through it all, I was communicating with Sonia. The thought that my folks knew where I was going and kept their distance did not matter to me anymore. I read and signed the consent forms. I really could not connect with the present situation or what I was doing. I think my mind went blank to keep me from the trauma of it all.

I went up to a room where they asked me to take off all my clothes and wear a hospital gown. I sent for the doctor and hoped that I could ask him to reconsider. When he got there, the look in his eyes said it all. He knew what I was going to ask, he could see the tears in my eyes trying not to roll down my face, but just assured me that the doctor he got was an expert and that all would be well.

Even though I had signed the papers, the doctor to procure the abortion asked me again if I was sure this was what I wanted to do. I asked him what choice I had. He was the only person who seemed to understand, not because he said anything, but from the look in his eyes I could imagine the many abortions he had performed on girls. I came to him desperate with no other choice. They put me on a stretcher and wheeled me into the theatre. They put my legs up on stirrups and began getting me ready. I asked him if he would wait till I was under the influence of the drugs to touch me. It was just him and another male assistant, which made me feel violated and I was glad I would not be awake to see them and feel them touch me and insert their crude instruments into me.

I had grown accustomed to anaesthesia, but for the first time, I was scared. I was shaking and my face was wet with tears. I did not know I had been shedding tears. As they pumped the drug into my veins, it felt like cold death creeping into me and I prayed for the first time in years, out loud even as the drug was taking effect.

"Our father, who art in heaven, hallowed be thy name, thy king...dom... co... me..." I said.

I woke up to the sound of the two men laughing and talking politics. I was told everything went well. I was later given instructions on what to do next. I did not hear a word. All I could think about was that they had told me that the killing of my child had gone well. I could not wrap my head around how such a barbaric thing could have gone "well".

I fell asleep and woke up when I felt someone move my legs. It was the male assistant who was in the theatre with the doctor. He was putting a sanitary towel in place because of the bleeding. When he was done, he looked me dead in the eye and said, "Keep this as is ... I hope now *utaacha kumangana ovyo.*" (I hope you will now stop sleeping around).

I had just lost a child. I wonder what he would think if I told him the great and reputable doctor was the one who got me pregnant.

I wanted to leave, and even though I was not ready to walk, I got up, got dressed and left. They got a hold of me as I stumbled out of the gate almost passing out and took me back in to rest.

The doctor who got me pregnant took me to a friend's house as he had a family member over and had no room for me. It was just around the time of the post-election violence in early 2008 and his people had been displaced and had sought refuge with him. I felt abandoned and alone.

All this was happening when I was at my job at a TV station. This was after I had recovered from depression. Halima was one of my good friends then. I remember how, after the procedure, I could not go home and she had no idea what I had just done.

I recall being so hungry and having to walk with her to town to get food. As I stood in line I felt my shoes get wet. I looked and it was blood. I knew we had to get out of there and make it back before I passed out and made a mess everywhere and thankfully we did. I turned my phone off as I did not want him or Sonia calling to ask if I was alright and having to pretend I was. I also did not want to talk about it.

The next day, I thanked my friend and went home where we pretended it never happened other than my dad asking me if I had taken care of the situation. We pretended so well that the very same week I was cleaning out some old baby things and my mum told me that I should keep some for the next baby I would have. For a moment I thought she was insane but it was not the first time she had said something so insensitive. I concluded that she was either insane or she was just evil.

I grieved for the entire year after that. Regardless of my situation, I had every right to grieve because I had lost my child. Being caught between a rock and a hard place is not much of a choice and whichever I chose would have a lifetime price to pay.

There are those that will argue that life begins after birth, I believe it starts at conception. Why else would we need antenatal care? Why would it not be alright for a pregnant woman to smoke and drink and do drugs? Why do we care so much for the unborn child if it's not even a life?

Having had an abortion does not mean I endorse the procedure. I love life and though mine has been one way, I know that it can turn around. I also know that not every child will go through what I did and turn out the way I did. I know that every child conceived has the right to be born and to live.

To those that may think this is a means to an end, I can assure you it is not. It may end the situation you now find yourself in which is pregnancy, but it will be the beginning of a whole new situation. I cannot tell you what to choose, I cannot tell your parent and boyfriends what to do, but I can say this, we are held prisoner or set free by the choices we make, so choose wisely.

To the society and those that judge, point fingers, and so on, I can assure you that none of us is innocent in this matter. We all play a role in seeing and ensuring that more and more girls walk into the clinics or to some back street butcher. We are not ready to teach our children and talk about sex and safe sex, but we are so ready to tear them down when they stumble in the dark and get pregnant. We have to come together on these matters.

When I told the doctor that I was expecting, his reaction remains permanently etched in my memory. He cursed! He held his head and scratched it as he wondered how it happened. Here was a doctor and he was asking how? How did he pass his medical examination? I had tried every type of contraceptive and wound up using the coil which got me ill and had to take it out. He had access to whatever pills I needed yet he always forgot. Regardless of this, I took most of the blame. I suppose women really play 90% of the role in getting themselves pregnant or at least that's how people make it appear. It has been that way for way too long and it really needs to change. I know that if we allowed the men to take their share of responsibility in the matter, they would be just as careful.

If you are like me, rest assured that there is nothing unforgivable with God. I did what I did, but I am still loved, accepted and blessed. No one can tell me otherwise. For a long time, I thought when the time came to have kids, I would be punished by not being able to bear kids, but I know that is not how God works because God is not like men. You are forgiven and you are blessed. You will have that wonderful spouse and marriage and healthy beautiful children. He does not add insult to injury. He blesses what should be cursed and mends what was broken.

Chapter 13
My Mirror

Many times people ask me how I came to find God and I really cannot take any credit for it. I never found God because I was never looking for Him. He found me. I had lost everything, including my mind and now I had lost my child. It seemed as though everything around me was calling out for death.

The beginning of 2008 was by far my worst year yet. Just a few days into the New Year, I had gone into a hospital and had the abortion. I kept wondering to myself if the baby had been a girl. Angel is what I would have called her. I recall the day I heard her heart beat and got the first glimpse of her. She was tiny, so so tiny that you almost could not tell she was there. You couldn't actually tell because the pregnancy was not showing.

The country was still reeling from the 2007/8 post-election violence and in some places, it still persisted. Many people had been displaced from their homes. The term IDPs, that is, Internally Displaced Persons, was now used on all the major stations. I worked for a local TV station at the time. I got to watch the breaking news more often than I would have preferred.

At one point, my crew and I had to go out to the Jamhuri Showgrounds, where one of the IDP camps was set up, to do a story. I had never seen anything like it. Was this what greed could do? Was this what humans were capable of?

I met a little girl who told me that she was there with her neighbour. The girl was from one tribe and her neighbour was from an opposing tribe. Even through the media was talking about how tribalism was the cause of everything, right there, I could see something different. The little girl told me that she was asleep when she woke up to her mother's screams and the chaos that surrounded her as strange men were breaking things apart and setting their house on fire. The last words she heard from her mother were for her to run and get away. As she was running, her neighbour took her and together with her children, they managed to get away and make it to the camp where they were now safe. She had not seen her mum, brother or any of her family again since that day.

It was hard for me to believe that this was happening in my country. At my home, all was well and peaceful although we would watch what was happening on TV along with the rest of the world.

This visit to the camp was the closest I had come to it all. I met a lady who was staying in one of the cattle sheds who had been shot. I had never seen a gunshot wound before nor had I ever seen one that was not even tended to.

She was shot near the shoulder and the bullet went right through and left a gaping hole. Seeing that changed my perspective of what I always saw in the movies. I knew that a bullet could cause harm, but I never imagined the power it had to rip apart the human flesh. It is something I only hope to forget. For a moment, I stopped and looked at all these people, homeless, wounded and lost. I thought of the ones who had died and how they had died and I remembered Atem, David and Gladys. David and Gladys were my high school mates from Rwanda.

Memories of the stories they told of genocide and war flashed before me at that moment. It seemed like it was happening here too. I was suddenly glad I had the abortion. I was glad that Angel would never have to live in a world like this where people butchered one another.

It had only been about two weeks after the unfortunate procedure at the hospital. I can't be sure, but I am guessing that's how long it should have taken for me to recover after an abortion. I received a call from the doctor who got me pregnant asking me to go over and see him. I made a decision at that moment never to let any man touch me again in the name of love unless he married me first. Since I never pictured myself getting married, I was secure in knowing I would never have to deal with men again.

It was a tough time. Work was getting more and more tedious to deal with and I was grieving inwardly. I did not have someone I could really share what I was feeling with. I know I had Sonia but there are times when you just want someone who has been where you are; someone who understands how one could end up so messed up.

As much as I loved Sonia, it was not always easy to tell someone so "perfect" about your mistakes. I know that no one is perfect, but Sonia was a saint in comparison to me. There were just some things we will never be able to understand each other on regardless of how much we love to support each other through them.

I recall getting more and more tired as the days rolled by. The doctor and I were still together and pretending to be great although I avoided him as much as I could. I did not really care too much about meeting his needs. I knew there was no way a man like him would have no one to cater for what he was not getting from me. I was not mad at him either. He was an atheist, a scientist, and according to him all I got rid of was a bunch of cells. I guess ignorance truly is bliss.

I was totally unmotivated and uninspired and I was growing very tired of people. I hated having to come to work and smile for the cameras. I hated waking up in the morning. I was just tired and felt undeserving of life. Everything had finally fallen in on me and the abortion seemed to be the straw that broke this camel's back.

I recall waking up on this particular day and I was happy. I was excited. I went to work and did everything as I should have and more, I was in a good mood, I did my scripts in an exceptional way and even spent some time with my friends after work. I got home and chilled out with my son and things seemed great. Not long after I went into my bathroom where I took out a razor and some pills and stood in front of the mirror, finally, happy and at peace that it was all going to end soon.

I took a handful of pills and popped them into my mouth and swallowed them. I was going to wait and run a bath, get in and slit my wrists and speed it all up. I was sure that if one way would not work another would. I had planned to take my life and I had every intention to succeed. I had no reason not to as I had researched how to do so on the internet. It is amazing what you can find online. As I searched, I wondered why anyone would put that kind of information online and how they allowed it to go there, but at the same time, I was just grateful that someone had. The pills were down and the water was running to fill the tub and I waited patiently knowing it was the last time I would ever have to.

I looked in the mirror one last time. I looked to see the girl I no longer recognized and longed to say goodbye to. As I looked into my eyes I could still see me, but as I looked at me I was looking at a stranger. Right then, something unbelievable happened. So unbelievable that, there are times I am afraid to tell the story for fear of being rendered mad. I heard a voice, as clear as day. It was not alarming for me to hear voices. After all, I had been diagnosed with Schizophrenia at some point. I had just not heard the voices in a long long time.

What was unbelievable was that this time, I knew who the voice belonged to. I never knew God as such. I mean we were not buddies, but without a doubt, even though I had never heard Him before I knew it was His voice. I was in awe that did not last long and I was quickly angered by the words He spoke.

"If you kill yourself, I will hold you accountable."

I was vexed. "You show up now, after all this time, at the end and you want to hold me accountable for ending what you never cared to save?"

I was so mad that I was crying and did not even realise it until I saw my tears drop to the sink below the mirror.

"Accountable for what? My life? You call this a life? Where were you when I needed you, when I called to you as a little girl? Where were you then, when you could have done something and I could still have had a chance at some sort of a life? You're not God, you are a coward."

The room fell silent. I spoke again, "I have nothing and I am nothing, what good am I to you? If you are such a merciful loving God why not just let me die in peace?"

He spoke again, "Give me nothing and I'll give you everything."

I stopped crying for a moment and I was shocked. What in the world was He talking about? I thought about what He said and I knew for a fact that nothing could come of me and I figured, since everyone else had failed and I had failed, why not just let Him have a go and fail too, what have I got to lose? I made a deal with God. I told Him I would take up His offer, but that if nothing had changed in three months, not only would He allow me to kill myself, but I would get a free pass into heaven. It's funny that although I did not see His face and heard only a voice, it's as though I could hear or feel him smile at what I said.

I washed my face. It had not been long after I had taken the pills so I just stuck my finger down my throat to induce a gag reflex and I also had a bath. I think the bath was more to give me time for what had just happened to sink in or at least if I was dreaming, it would help wake me up. I did not share with anyone what had happened till a while later. I did not know what to say and if people would believe me, I was not sure I believed it myself.

I had spent time with Muslims and I chose to fast as they did for 30 days. I would start at six and break at six. The first day was hard. I was in the habit of smoking at least 2 packets of cigarettes a day and I could not wait for six to have a smoke. I never prayed. I just went right into my smoke at six and it felt so good. Again I heard the voice.

"I will meet with you every day at this time, and all I ask is that when you come before me, you do not do it with a cigarette in hand. Give me just the 30 days you have put aside and after that you can go back to smoking."

I knew it would be hard, but when it came down to it, it was not. Every day at six, we would meet and talk. It was never about anything from the Bible really or from church but everything else: the flowers, the trees and the sky. It was like being introduced to nature and the world again only this time by the creator. I was filled with a peace that I cannot understand or explain and before I knew it, the 30 days were over. The strange thing is that I forgot that I smoked and never picked up another stick again. By the time of writing this book, it had been 8 years since I touched a cigarette.

People ask me how I just stopped smoking. I realised that to try and quit anything is a waste of time. To try and stop smoking will only lead to you to start drinking. Instead of stopping, ask yourself why you do it. I smoked because I suffered from anxiety. I seemed to be in a place of constant restlessness and fear, worry and so I smoked to calm myself down. What I got in place of my anxiety was peace, calm, stillness and with that I had no need for a smoke. I just needed to step outside, watch the trees and flowers and be still.

One may ask what happened to me after three months and all I can say is that He never failed me and never has. This is not just something I am saying because it's the cliché thing that a believer should say; I am saying it as an individual bearing witness daily to it. There are people out there who confuse being a believer and being a Christian or belonging to a religion, but it's not the same thing. Many Christians are born into that religion. It is the religion of their father and mother, going to church on their worship day is what the family does. Regardless of what happens on other days, worship day morning will find them in church because they are Christians.

Being a believer for me has nothing to do with being a Christian. Personally, I cannot give you a clear definition of what Christianity is or who is a Christian. There is a lot of confusion in religion. I know that confusion is not God's character. Religion has been at the heart of many terrible acts against humanity in the name of God. Men and women of God have done many ungodly things in the name of God and we know that, we see them on television calling you to send in money in exchange for a miracle, to buy some holy water, to give them something in return for a child, a husband, money and so many other things. I am not talking about religion, religion chewed me up and I had to crawl out of its jaws before it completely devoured me.

I speak of God of love. A love that allows me to look in the mirror and love what I see even though I don't look the part. I look and see some dimples, some stretch marks, scars. I see a woman; I see a black woman; I see a single mum; I see someone who never graduated from university and I look beyond that and see God. I see what Christ did for me. I look at myself in the mirror and what I see is **a crown of beauty for ashes**. Beloved as I am so can you be and as I AM so YOU ARE.

Chapter 14
My Redeeming Love

Many years after high school, I never completely forgot about my friend Atem. He was always somewhere, at the back of my mind, lingering in my thoughts.

Atem was born on July 7th 1980. He was born in Sudan which is currently South Sudan. He was, to others, a surprisingly big baby. They all were, but if you have known a Dinka man or woman you will know that many of them are very tall and I guess it starts right from birth. The manner in which both he and Sonia have impacted my life goes to show me that God had made plans for me in advance. He had put people in place that I would come to meet and be changed through even before I was born.

His father and many great men and women came together to fight for the freedom of their people as they formed the SPLA (Sudan People's Liberation Army)/SPLM (Sudan People's Liberation Movement). Many of his people have seen death and loss. They have seen what human beings can do to one another for the sake of power. We often hear about the child or boy-soldiers but never can we imagine their lives, never can we imagine them having to flee on foot from their war-torn country and destroyed homes and having to take refuge in a foreign land.

From a young age, Atem's family was forced to live as refugees in neighbouring nations. When I met him in the high school we attended, he would often speak in Spanish with a classmate called Ronaldo who was from Brazil. He would also speak to me in Spanish as he knew I loved the language even though I did not understand it. It was puzzling to see how he spoke the language fluently, but that is because he had been a refugee in Cuba as a child as were many children from Sudan at the time.

Life was never ordinary for Atem. He battled many things that none of us would imagine growing up and even as adults. When I would sit and listen to him tell stories, I would be astonished at what he had had to endure, but, I would also see a baby; a boy, a child and a man who beat the odds to become what he is.

We would spend hours on the phone in high school talking and more hours in school doing the same. Back then, not many people had seen people that looked like Atem. To the girls, he was not worth their time. He was not light-skinned and built like some of the others were, and when he spoke, it was mainly about art, history and people. He was not what people would call interesting. It was not that he was not interesting, but that he had real things to talk about, and not the latest in pop culture and such. We had our moments with all that, and I recall introducing him to one of my favourite hip hop artists at the time, The Wu Tang Clan, but all in all, we were different from the others.

People would talk behind his back and call his father all manner of things. I did not know much about his father then, but one thing I did know was that he was not what people said he was. I do know that when it comes to war, freedom comes at a high price and not everyone will understand why it has to be done. The world would much rather sit and be comfortable forgetting that somewhere in a country are a people enslaved and oppressed, but take up arms and fight for liberty and you will have people say things about you.

Atem and I had a very strong and deep bond, but it never went beyond school and friendship. When I graduated from high school, I never kept in touch with anyone, not even Atem. I recall being homesick and thinking about him and wondering where he was. I figured Atem would go back and join his father in the war.

Life out of high school became very real for me and my girlie fantasies about my Dinka prince became just that: a fantasy.

Many terrible and brilliant things happened between the day I left Atem in high school and the day we met again. I thought he had died. I thought he went back and was killed in the war. Perhaps my mind was just used to terrible things and all it could conjure up was that. If there was one thing I had learnt to do from a very early stage in my life was to never hope or expect any good thing.

I dared not hope or expect anything, when I walked into the Java House on Koinange Street, Nairobi on the afternoon of February 6th, 2011 to meet Atem. In fact, I believed it was a one-time meeting. We would catch up and head back our separate ways. Fate however, had other things planned.

Ours is a story so unreal that I still think I was dreaming. I never in a million years could have thought of the things that came after I walked into that coffee house, and I think the best place to start would be at the beginning.

In 2011, I had a dream about my old friend Atem. He was being crowned king and he asked me to stand by him as his queen. I began to walk up the steps to take my place by his side and though to many this would be a sweet dream, it put such fear in me that it jolted me out of the dream. After all that had happened to me from the time I was a child, I had come to the conclusion that there were those to whom life was just sweet because that's how it was written and those whom life was just bitter and that's where I fell. I dared not to dream and expect or even hope that love, a man or marriage was in my cup.

After God found me, I stopped hating men. Indeed, I had seen and known many good men. Some were my teachers, some were my friend's husbands and there was always Atem who had always been good to me.

I was sweating, and my heart was racing as I prayed. It had been many years since we had seen each other. I had bumped into him once, but at the time, my life was in such a ruin that I was ashamed of what I had turned out to be and I did not want him to see or know me for what I had become. In high school, I never shared with him the things that happened to me.

Although I'd been to hell and back, I still had a tiny ember of hope that maybe one day I could find a man, fall in love and get married. In high school though we were just friends, a thought did dance through my mind that maybe one day it would be him. He never said anything and I never asked, after all it was high school.

After the dream, I could not help but look for him.

My search led me to his cousin who pointed me in the right direction. He was going under a different name. I sent him a message on Facebook.

Dear Atem,

It is June from high school. You may not remember me. Anyway, I thought of looking you up and finding out how you are and what you have been up to.

I had no expectations however. Later in the day I got a response from him.

Do I remember you? I never forgot. I have thought about you all these years and looked for you but could not find you. You changed your names?

I noted with delight that he did not live in Kenya. The farther away he was the less likely he was to see me.

Yes I changed my names. I see here that you live in Juba, I am in Nairobi. I hope you are all well. I hope one day we will get to meet again. Take care. I finished.

He replied back telling me that he had landed in Nairobi the night before, the night I had the dream. My heart skipped a few beats then sunk and then danced. I gave him my number, he called me and we planned to meet.

On February 6th 2011, we met at the Java House in town. I was glad to see him, and he looked even more handsome than I remembered. He was a lot bigger too. I tried not to give it much thought because I had learnt by now that hope was not to be played around with. I simply wanted to find out why I needed to look for him so that God could tell me what I needed to pray or say over him and leave. I was there on assignment and nothing more. He gave me a gift, a book – *Negro with a Hat*. It was just like him to do that.

To avoid disappointment, I decided that this was a goodbye gift.

That one thing about us had not changed. I told him about my dream and his response surprised and annoyed me. He told me that he had loved me in high school and still did.

"I have been looking for you for years now. I promised myself that if I ever found you again, I would not be silent like I was then. I loved you then and I love you still. I am not afraid to say it because I have come to learn that tomorrow is not promised," Atem said.

The nerve of the man! I wanted to take the bottle on the table and crack it over his head. Did he not know where I was coming from? How could he tell me this now? Maybe if he told me in high school my life would be different, could he not see I was spent? Could he not see that I was done with people and I had now chosen to live for God? Could he not see that even though part of me had always wanted to hear that, it completely broke what was left of me? What good was I now? I had nothing more to give. I was damaged goods. I was God's property now and God loved me. No man ever could or would love me and I wished he would save me the lies. I was so angry. I did not know what was going on. I was so hurt by his words. I was so angry and I was fighting back tears. It felt like a joke. Twelve years later and now he was sitting there telling me the things I longed to hear then that I could dare not believe in now. For a moment, I felt like I used to when I thought God had put me in this life to play games for His own delight.

It was 1pm when we met at Java House. We talked till it shut down. We then walked to another place that was open late and talked some more. He asked about my brother, we all schooled together and when we called my brother, he invited us to his place. We stayed there catching up till 3 am. My brother took me home, while Atem took a taxi to his home.

We continued to meet after that day. After all, God had not told me or shown me anything yet and I figured as we talked I would know why I was there. The more he claimed to love me, the angrier I got. How could he love me? Men did not love me, men lusted over me, and moreover, he was not saved so I judged for myself that he and I could not be.

Now that I think about it, my religion was what I used to keep most people out. I see now that I used my religion as a justification to reject him and keep him from getting too close. I did not see it at the time, but religion had become my new wall. He, however, was the most persistent and relentless man I had ever known. He would not be shaken off, give up or just vanish no matter how hard I turned him down. Many were surprised that I was being the way I was to him; they thought he was kind, loving and gentle. He had never been cruel to me, nor was he anything but gentle with me, but that he was a man, meant he was extremely dangerous and I thought that at any moment, given the opportunity, he could be the death of me. I did not want him to see me and yet all he wanted to do was get closer.

I tried to justify my bailing out of this situation with my religion, but it seemed even God would not release me to leave or walk away. All I could feel for Atem, no matter how hard I fought, was love. I wanted to love him but how? This by far was the most difficult thing for me to do. To make it worse, everyone loved him: my parents, my friends, even my son and yet, I could not look past my fear of him seeing what I had been through. He would tell me that he was not like the others, but I could not let go of my fear to trust him. I realised I could not let go and trust God.

With time, I managed to bring out everything about my past and he managed to see what I hid from him. But instead of rejecting me, instead of using me as others had, he loved me. He loved me in spite of it and for some unexplainable reason I fought it. I told God that I was scared to lose him, but at the same time scared of what was happening to me.

One day, God asked me to give him my Isaac just the way the Biblical Abraham did. To give him this man and the promise of the love and marriage that came with it, I did, but it was not easy.

Soon after, he came into town. At this point he hated me, my lack of trust; my inability to receive his love had taken its toll. I realised yet again that all my life, I gave love and loved in order to get but never got anything in return and as a result, I never knew how to be loved, I never knew how to let this man just love me.

The last time I saw him, he pointed out my rings, rings that I had got from others in my past and moreover the one from Sally. He looked at me and asked how he, being a man, could ever find room to place his ring when the time came when all I carried was my past? He reminded me of the lesbian relationship I was once in and he pointed out how I still wore her ring. I excused myself and went into the bathroom where I took off my rings and disposed all of them. I knew that something had to give, I was not sure how I was going to do it, but I knew it had to be done.

The night ended well. He left town the following day. As he left, I was reminded of words he spoke to me. He had told me that the future was unknown to him, but he was willing to embrace it. On that day I opened myself to the unknown knowing that God had never failed me and he never would.

That was the last I heard from him for a while. At first I was hurt. I thought because I had hurt him, he was punishing me like others had done in my past. I then caught myself drifting back into my past. I also realised that he had been true to his word and had never acted like any man I had ever known. Again, I thought he had found some girl out there who could give him all that I could not. In all honesty, my not sleeping with Atem was not because I was a Christian, sex had gone out through the window long before God came into the picture, but using religion was a good way to avoid it. I had never loved a man other than Atem. I had never been sexually attracted to any man other than Atem and I had never made love to any man I loved and even though I wanted to, I didn't know how to make love to Atem whenever the time came. I was so afraid of disappointing him.

I thought that this was the end for me and even Atem, but it was just the beginning.

Chapter 15
My Religion

I figured that since I had found God and salvation, I now needed to find the religion that goes with it. Naturally, when we get saved, or experience salvation, church is what comes next. I got into the church I was now attending because it is where I would get counselling for my grief. I was still with the doctor, and I was still grieving the loss of my child. I liked this church because they did not question the way I looked. I also liked it because I was a totally new face. I knew no one and no one knew of me other than Sonia who attended this congregation. It had a young congregation and the pastors seemed accommodating to everyone. I also liked the music.

As time passed, I found myself feeling more and more at home in the church. I had lost so much and now I had found something and so I gave it all I had. I did not feel out of place or rejected and that was great. The church taught a lot about prosperity and marriage. I did not mind so much the idea of living long and prospering, but I was not too keen on marriage. I found a media team that I joined and felt like I was part of, yet something was still not all there for me. I still found myself having to be different to fit in and then it felt like people liked me not because I was one of them, but because I was the cool chic. I was artsy, edgy and that intrigued to them.

When you stay in a place long enough, you start to see the cracks in the wall, and I did. I found myself not focusing on God as much as on the pastors, prosperity and marriage. I became increasingly uncomfortable. But I was not alone, Sonia felt it too. I would come to meet all manner of people in the congregation. I met some men who invited me over to their house to watch pornographic films, the very same men whose wives were trying to get to know me better.

There is nothing wrong with teaching about prosperity and marriage. I know that God wants us to succeed in life. God also said it is not good for man to be alone, but being single is not that big a deal either. All the girls talked about marriage and all the boys talked about getting rich. We were always giving, but hardly ever receiving. It was evident that at the end of the day, what I was dealing with was not a church as such but a business and I was not getting any return on my investment.

I eventually stopped attending that church. Many things happened that I care not to mention, but the bottom line is that I had had enough. Offering, tithe, seed, pledges... it just never ended. Meanwhile, the pastors; their pockets, cars and houses seemed to get bigger, mine were getting thinner.

Sonia and I soon found a new church and it was quite different. The message they taught was really deep and I liked that because it reminded me of the first 30 days I spent fasting. It was really about getting closer and closer to God and that was great. It was very different in that the atmosphere was very uptight and it was not long before I began to get uncomfortable again. I had come from a place where people were quite free to sing and dance and do other things, but here it seemed alien. This church did not teach about prosperity. It seemed like they feared it actually, and so it was on the very opposite end of the other one. Here, being 'cool' and so different was not very acceptable either and I stood out like a sore thumb.

For the first time, I had to think about what to wear or not to wear to church. It got to a point that if I had nothing to wear I would stay at home because if I did show up with say a sleeveless top, I would be made to cover up or sit outside. Again it felt like I had to work so hard and be something I am not to fit in. I was glad that in both churches I got a lot of teachings and great music, but I found myself lost as to what I was supposed to be or what I had to do for me to fit in. There is a very big difference between being religious and being ungodly. I understand dressing in modesty, but there is a place where it can be taken overboard.

I found a job on the media team of a Christian organization that taught people how to apply God's word in business. It was nice. The people were friendly and easy going. Too easy going, actually. They had such a 'good old time' and it almost felt like heaven on earth. There was something about the place that felt off, but I could not put my finger on it.

When working behind the scenes, you get to see a lot of what people hide when they get on stage or in front of a camera. My new job was no different. The class teacher made it appear as though we were one big, close happy family, but in reality, he was never around apart from the one day a week to teach. The students would ask me about him and I would tell them that I only got to see him when he was teaching. The organization felt like a love child he had with someone, he took care of it, but never cherished it as such.

Many things were not adding up. For a place that once again taught about God and prosperity and the man in charge claiming to be a millionaire, we were pretty lacking. I recall not being paid on time and my rent becoming an issue. When I called him, he promised to sort things out and I came to find out that we were the lucky ones as others in his other businesses had not been paid for months. Money problems were definitely evident.

I came to learn too that members of staff were not to question the way things were run and my not being one to shut up was not something that they liked. This man may as well have been a god the way everyone idolised him.

At the time, I was considering Atem's proposal. He could see that things were not right at my workplace.

Eventually, I quit my job. I had to find something that was going to pay me on time. My dad had given me some money as a loan for my rent that I would repay when we finally got paid to avoid getting evicted. Enough was enough. The last pay was said to be delayed. But it never came in the end.

I went on to finally join another Christian organization that not only allowed me to write in their paper, but would give me a chance to sell a television show that I was working on. What I realised about this place early enough was that they avoided signing any agreements with me, and used the word of God to assure me they were righteous and full of integrity. I was not buying it so I chose to only do work that I got paid for upon delivery, and work that I could stop doing at any given time. It's important that Christians learn to operate businesses in a professional manner. Prayer and quoting the Bible is not a binding agreement. If anyone, Christian or otherwise, is not willing to go about business the right way, steer clear of them or move with caution.

I was also working with a Christian lady on my television show, and that was going well. She, too, had this tendency of not signing anything and as such I chose to secure my intellectual property through copyright as I had lost my life story to a movie once that way. I thank God I did because when she tried to sell the show, she was caught with her pants down and could not carry on.

I came to confirm, as the Bible says, that there are false prophets. The people we sometimes see on the pulpit are not always the real deal. Not every man and woman who will stand on the pulpit quoting scripture is sincere. Granted, the church is an organization and they are allowed to do certain things to make money to keep their day to day needs met and that is where our tithes and offering comes in. But that does to translate to the extravagant needs of the pastors. Some false prophets can use sweet words to manipulate their congregation.

I also came to realise that there is a difference between religion and Godliness. Only when we break free from religious rituals, acts, rules, regulations and laws can we fully appreciate God's grace.

When we place all manner of rules and regulations on people, are we not just undoing what He did? Are we not missing the point of salvation?

So we can pray ten times a day, wear the longest robes, cover our hair, attend church every day of the week, but at the end of it all, none of our deeds will get us to the Father.

I had been so carried away and lost in religion and religiousness, I lost the place to grace, the place of Christ in my life. I was reminded of the teachers of religious law that were all about doing but not being. I spent all of 2012 breaking free from it all, breaking away from deeds to grace, understanding salvation and what Christ did on the cross, understanding that we are all one that are called by His name.

Today I do go to church. It is still the only place that can teach me what I need to know. I don't throw the baby out with the bath water and I ask that you do not either. It is up to us to seek truth beyond what we hear on the pulpit or on television and wherever else. Don't get second hand information. Don't have a go-between when you already have direct access to God.

When asked what religion I belong to, I am not ashamed or afraid to say none. I am a believer in God, in Christ and a follower of his teachings, but I do not fit into any label or box associated with any religion, opinion or views other than the truth. It is sad that the church is so divided, that people are so segregated. We have so many religions founded on truth, but separated by views and opinions.

Christians cannot even agree amongst themselves nor can many others. The many views and opinions of the men and women in power distort the image of truth so many people cannot see it. Truth is not something that is taught, it is something that is revealed to you, and the only way to know it is to seek it. Seek God and his kingdom. Know the truth and the truth shall set you free.

I recall in school when one of my friends got pregnant out of wedlock and was terrified because her father would kill her, literally. She had to be sent to live in another country where she had her child that was passed as her sister or something so that her father would never know and therefore not kill her because in her religion it happened.

We have heard and also witnessed the amount of pressure that is placed on pastor's children to somehow be perfect as though that could ever be achieved. Is that fair? Someone could say, "I can't believe he was smoking, and he is the pastor's son." Religion does not exempt us from our human imperfections, or trials. So many times I hanged out with girls who would leave the house dressed in what their religion required, all covered up only to take it all off and toss it aside once they were out. I also witnessed some girls who had fallen into sexual acts before marriage and because their religion required that they be virgins before marriage, they chose instead to have anal sex so that they would go undetected when the day and time came.

I came to learn while training to be a counsellor, that there is such a thing as spiritual abuse, where a child is expected to act and be in a certain spiritual way that is way beyond their capability and age. Some of the children who undergo such demands in the religious and spiritual arena may rebel in the worst way, and in many cases abandon God all together.

It is our job as parents to teach and train our children. When a child does not believe in God, as I didn't, gently find out why. If a child has questions about God, help them with answers if you know. If you do not know, be honest. It allows the child to know that there is room for growth and imperfection, room for them to seek for themselves. Children have minds of their own. They have thoughts and feelings. They are people and we need to recognise that. "Because I said so" is not sufficient and especially in this case where a child needs is seeking clarification about God.

Allow the child to feel that they are free to question, free to research and learn, free to choose; and help them make the right choice. Do not force them. When we do things in love, it wins them over, but when we push, we could push them away.

Chapter 16
My Catalyst

As I read through the introduction of the book *The Power of Now* by Eckhart Tolle, something he mentioned triggered a reaction within me. He wrote that he hoped that his book would act as a catalyst for radical inner transformation.

Atem was a great catalyst for my awakening and being the conscious being I now am. One lesson I'll never forget came about at one point when we were watching cartoons at Atem's house with his family and my son, when his mother walked in and asked to watch the news.

"Shobe, Cucu wants to watch the news. It's time to change the channel," I told him.

"Oh, but mum I don't want to watch news, it's boring and I don't understand it. I want to watch cartoons," he responded.

I was quick to say, "Listen to your elders."

Atem's mother cut in and said, "No, no, let him watch. I will watch the evening news."

At that moment, my son realised that his preferences too were important and perhaps more important than the news.

I was introduced to a new society. A society where people thought differently, where people are free to be themselves and where every individual is valued regardless of sex, race and religion. I was also introduced to a new earth through a great teacher and writer Eckhart Tolle who allowed me to further awaken to the thing that had been started, with Atem. I know that I am a being; I am not my sex, my race, my achievements or my religion. I will not be squeezed into any box to make people feel better, more comfortable or make them accept me.

Atem was able to love me and help me in a way in which the godly folk did not and could not. God works in mysterious ways and to ever think you know Him or know everything would be a mistake because He showed me that he can use anything and anyone.

I am a believer but I was blinded by religion and it took someone to open my eyes.

It is not our job to know how God works but to believe and I do. I believe that as His word says: it is not good for man to be alone and He created woman to be a companion, a suitable helper and equal and that I am, and agree to be, to the man he has placed in my life. How it will work, only God knows, mine is to make myself available, and answer the call which I have. I have chosen to this day to stand by Atem, not trusting in my own ways to do so, but looking to God to guide me. To be used by God, to be the helper and companion He created me to be, and to be all that in His time for in His time all things are beautiful.

I have learnt from Atem's late father, a man who fought for Sudan's freedom, that perfect love does cast out fear. His love for family, his people, and his country overcame his fear of death and he was able to lay down his life for it. He and many others; for the love of his people, for the love of freedom and to him and to the men and women that fell, I salute.

To Atem's family and to his late father, I say thank you, without you, being used to bring Atem to be, my life would never have been the same. Without you instilling in him the things he has, without raising him to be the man that he is and still will be, my life and that of many more to come would never be the same.

To Atem, know that you have all it takes to be all you were created to be. I pray that you never doubt yourself, never let fear keep you from greatness and know that I believe in you and support you always. You are and always will be the love of my life. I forgive my ignorance and imperfections and any hurt I may have caused, that we may come to fulfill our destiny together as it was meant to be. I pray for your happiness and moreover the fullness of your greatness and that God may allow me to be there with you to witness it.

Chapter 17
Fight for Me

It is not with lack of gratitude that I write this one chapter. I acknowledge and appreciate the fight, the effort and the work many people and organizations have taken up to ensure that children, women and human beings in general have rights.

I think about that child I used to be and even though I went through what I did, I am happy that others like her have rights that can protect them. I think about the teenage girl I was, drugged and raped and I am glad that it is not something that is tolerated. I think about Atem and his people, the stories I heard of children taking up arms to fight, children being abducted to be killers against their will. Human beings used and sold as slaves, some even sex slaves and I am grateful that there are those who do not turn a blind eye, that there are those who make sure that we have rights.

I saw on the news once about a girl who had been raped. She was only nine years old and her father, instead of having to deal with the shame it would bring, opted to marry her off to the very man who raped her. I saw one like that too about a young girl in India. The ordeal was so bad and shameful that she even killed herself over it.

The culture, society and social environment is far more dangerous to a victim of sexual abuse at any age than the violators themselves. There is no atmosphere created for people like me to heal, to get support and get back to life. My silence and the silence of many, gives the abuser or rapist a chance to get away.

The system can only do so much, the organizations have done their bit and now I call upon people, families, schools, friends and the society at large to fight for us and with us.

It is so hard to fight the things that happened to us and still fight you and what you put us through. We become not just victims of abuse but of the social bashing and denial that comes with it.

If it is happening, we have to speak up. If you know anything you must raise the alarm. We have rights but what good are they if you won't fight for them with us and for us?

We cannot stop child abuse, sexual abuse through prison, we must, where possible, find the root of the abuse and stop it.

*****

My crown of beauty for ashes

The first thing we must always try to do is prevent bad things from happening. If we can prevent our children from being abused, violated, discriminated and so on, we will save ourselves a lot of work to mend them. Prevention has and always will be better than cure.

I am still healing from what happened to me as a child. All of it is becuase of what happened then and that is why I insist on protecting the children, fighting for them and championing for their rights. A healthy child grows into a healthy adult who makes healthy decisions that create a healthy world. Healthy children become healthy citizens not just of a community or nation but of the world. The world we are living in is a reflection of our state of health. It is much harder to fix a broken adult than to prevent a child from being broken. It may not always be possible but there is a way.

The book of Isaiah 61 talks about healing and restoration. This passage speaks to and about me more than any other. The spirit of the Lord is upon me, to bring good news to the poor, to comfort the broken hearted and to let you know that He can and will give a crown of beauty for your ashes.

Being burnt does not mean being out. Being broken and even shattered is not the end for you or me. In my case, it was the beginning of something amazing and big. It was the fire I had to go through to be the gold that is today. A friend of mine who is a teacher told me that gold does not burn or turn to ashes under fire, but is refined. I am gold and so are you beloved. The fire will burn. The ashes will fall so that the gold is revealed. There are many ways we go through this process of alchemy, but rest assured it is not to kill you but to bring glory.

What others say

"Thitu Kariba is not only a courageous lady but a person so committed to other people's growth at the expense of her own! When we go through what people consider shameful, we tend to shield ourselves from further shame by covering our own shame...but the more we cover, the more the pain. Thitu Kariba not only shares her life with close friends but also with us all. ..." *Julia Kagunda*

Last Word...
From My Son

My name is Shobe (Sholike Kariba Munio) and I want to tell you about my mum. I love my mum very much. She does a lot of things for me and she treats me well. She is kind to me. My mum is also a good speaker.

My mum is caring and responsible. She is kind to other people. I thank God that He gave me a mother like her. I am glad that she is my mother. When you see her, ask her how to be good. Please read and share this book, because it is very important to our lives.

Dear mum,

I love you very much and I am glad that you are kind and good to others. I wrote this letter because I like the way you have been good and faithful. Please continue like that, just the way you are good kind and responsible. I love you just the way you are.

From Shobe.

About the Author

Thitu Kariba, is known to many as *The Healing Ambassador*. She has been an instrument of restoration and reformation through various platforms. Her first-hand experience being a victim of child abuse and rape, her plunging into depression and her eventual recovery have led her to use her life story to bring about awareness and understanding.

Thitu shares from her real-life experiences. Her hope is to reach out to as many people as possible through all forms of media, including TV (as she does through her show *Beauty for Ashes*) and the written word, among others.

Thitu holds a Diploma in Mass Communication, and is certified both as a counselling psychologist and a zumba fitness instructor. She has worked for the Kenya Broadcasting Cooperation (KBC) as a TV show presenter/host, and as a guest speaker for Capital FM's 'After Hours' on healing and relationships. Further, she has written on relationships for the Capital Lifestyle Magazine, and maintains a blog and an online magazine on spiritual living. As a fitness instructor, Thitu completes the cycle of health that addresses physical health and wellbeing.